Opening Hearts

A Journey of Service and Transformation in China

by Susan Straight

Intercultural Education Publishing
237 Camino del Norte
Santa Fe, NM 87501
www.centerinterculturaled.org

Cover photos Susan Straight; Author photo: Karl Linaur; Cover and Back Cover Design: Patti Blair; Back Cover Photo: Susan Straight; Book Design: Susan Straight

Opening Hearts is a true story of actual events. The Names used are those of the actual participants in the program.

Printed in the United States of America
Library of Congress Cataloging-in-Publication Data
Straight, Susan
Opening Hearts, A Journey of Service and Transformation in China---
Santa Fe, NM: Intercultural Education Publishing 2016
ISBN-13: 978-15429116
ISBN-10: 154291166

1. Transformation, 2. Community Service, 3. Intercultural Education. 4. Empowerment, 5. NGOs, 6. Humanitarian Work

Table of Contents

Dedication

This book is dedicated to the young people of the world.
Through their open hearts,
their enthusiasm and creativity,
a new world will be created for all.

"I believe the children are our future,
teach them well and let them lead the way.
Show them all the beauty they possess inside. . ."

Foreword

This is a story about love, love for the young people of China searching for deep connection--

of the villagers, grannies and children.

This is a story of being moved deeply by ordinary things and of making a difference in the lives of total strangers.

One nature,
perfect and pervading,
circulates all natures.
One reality,
all-knowing,
contains with itself all realities.
The one moon is reflected
wherever there is a sheet of water;
And all the moons in all the waters
are embraced by the one moon.
The embodied truth of all the Buddhas
enters into my own being,
And in my own being is found union with theirs.

The inner light is beyond both praise and blame,
Like unto space it knows no boundaries;
Yet it is right here with us,
ever retaining its serenity and fullness.
It is only when you seek it that you lose it;
You cannot take hold of it nor can you get rid of it.
While you can do neither, it goes on its way.
You remain silent and it speaks;
you speak and it is silent.
The gate of heaven is wide open
with not a single obstruction before it.
Yung-chia Hsuan-chueh

Prologue

I awoke in the early dawn to total silence in this city of 6 million people, where I had come to heal a deeply wounded heart. I did not know what I would encounter here, only that I must come and find out.

It all began at the time of life when something new was needed, but this did not unfold in the way I had anticipated.

My husband Bruce and I had recently "retired" (in quotes because we didn't at all feel like we wanted a life of leisure). We were looking forward to creating the next phase of our lives. He wanted to focus on his photography, and I on my textile art. And then there was the first grandchild who had just arrived. On the surface, things looked wonderful, but in truth, I think we were a bit bored, disconcerted by the sudden loss of the stimulation of co-workers and the structure of work. My work had been self-directed for the past 10 years, and for much of it, I was out in the world, training teachers, working with the legislature to secure funding, and taking students out on service-learning trips. Now, we were both at home, direction-less in many ways.

Then, one day, quite out of the blue, Bruce received a phone call from an acquaintance we hadn't seen in many years. The acquaintance was in China, teaching English, and one of the expected new teachers had canceled at the last moment. He had had a dream in which he saw Bruce, and thinking that was a sign of some kind, he called to offer him the job. After Bruce hung up, we discussed this unexpected turn of events. It would mean a year in China, an exciting proposition for him—but what would I do there? We had traveled a lot in our 25 years together and were in love with parts of Asia, especially Japan, but neither of us had ever felt particularly drawn to China. Now this offer was on the table, a quick reply needed, and Bruce was clearly anxious to take it.

It was September 2004 when the phone call came, and my new grandson was just a month old. He was not really Bruce's grandson, but of course he was, as my son had grown up with him, being only 6 years old when we got together. Facing the fact that we were now grandparents had turned out to be more difficult than I would have ever imagined. Everyone I knew said that their grandchildren were the joys of their lives, but we were very young feeling and looking, and so it was an adjustment. I had to make a shift from the mental picture I had of "grandmother." That word conjured up a picture of my own grandmother, a white haired, slightly plump woman who taught me to cook pies, sew and knit, and whose life was completely dedicated to being a grandmother. That just wasn't me. And I think the idea of grand parenting was even worse for Bruce. He was only 62 at the time, and slightly obsessed with staying young—playing tennis several times a week, trying all kinds of vitamins and supplements. He didn't want to take on the role, and so he didn't. But when I held this new life in my arms, something magical happened. Even though I had doubts about my identity, I had no doubt about the love flowing between us.

And so the decision was made. I would stay home to help out during the first months of my grandchild's life, and Bruce would head off to China to teach. He would return at Christmas time, and we then would both go back to China in January.

i.

I could never have imagined then how this choice would change my life, but it did—drastically.

Though I have often wondered, I will never know how things might have turned out if I had gone with him. If I knew what was to happen, would I have made a different choice? For by the time he returned for Christmas, he had fallen in love with a Chinese woman 30 years his junior, and I was facing the loss of the deepest and most significant connection of my life.

Chapter 1

Three Visions

The Master observes the world
but trusts his inner vision.

The news Bruce brought home with him hit me very hard. I reeled from it, went through the full gamut of emotions: shock, grief, anger, self-pity, and despair. On the outside, I went through the motions. There was Christmas to get through, and all the logistics involved in separating our households. All the while, I was raw. I felt like a ship adrift on a windless sea. Through a deep fog, I reached for answers. And now, what am I to do?

And then, unbidden, three visions came.

The First Vision

I am sitting on the grass in Green Lake Park, looking at the beauty of the green trees, the water lilies and lotus blossoms. As I am sitting there, young people begin to gather around me until there are about 35 or 40 of them. They begin to speak in turn, each telling of a yearning in their heart, a yearning for meaning and connection. They are asking me how to have that in their lives. I am telling them about many of the most important and meaningful things in my own life. As they speak, I can feel an energy flowing between us, a feeling that speaks of all of us being deeply connected.

The Second Vision

I have gone to a village in China with a team of people to work. As we walk into the village, the head man steps forward to welcome all of us. As our eyes meet, it is very clear that we know each other at some deeper level. We all met to decide what is to be done, and as the other members of the team set to work on their various tasks, the headman asks to speak with me in his home. We sit on the floor around a table laden with food, and he begins to tell me that he has been waiting for me to come and is overjoyed that I have finally arrived. He has dreamed of me as I have dreamed of him. We have no difficulty understanding each other's language.

It is clear in my vision that this is a minority village, and the head man wants to talk to me about the struggles of the minority people in China. They are trying to keep their own cultures alive so as not to be completely absorbed into the mainstream culture. We talk about finding the essence of their culture, of how to awaken the knowledge of that essence in each member of the village, so that it might always be held in the heart. We talked about the value of the minority cultures and their villages, of their loving connection to the earth and to each other, of their spiritual connections.

The Third Vision

I have been taken to a school classroom. There is no teacher there, only a young girl of about 10 and a number of other children, all somewhat younger. They, too, tell me that they have been waiting for me to come to them. They wish to know about the purpose of life on earth, and to discover who they really are. They are very awake and alive, in touch with something very spiritual. They ask me to teach them about these things, that they might live lives of meaning and purpose. As with the older students, there is a feeling of deep connection.

These visions all came to me in that sweet time just before fully waking, when one is in a half awake-half dream state. I knew that at least the first two had taken place in China.

I had experienced visions before. They tended to come to me over the years whenever I was at a crossroads, and knew I needed to take a new direction. At these times, visions had provided much-needed signposts, pointing the way to the next part of my life. Visions, to me, are a kind of gift the Universe gives to us, and over the years I have learned to respect them and work with them. Whenever a vision comes, I see it as being given a glimpse of a world yet to manifest, a world that is wanting to come into being, and is seeking a channel, an agent, someone who can help bring it to fruition.

The last time I had been gifted with a vision of such detail was ten years before when I had just started my first non-profit. I was essentially shown the whole program, and how it would unfold over the next 3-4 years. This information was given to me in a format that ultimately became a strategic plan. I only had to sit down at the computer and let it be written through me. I then proceeded to implement it in the time frame that had been given to me.

I had learned that there is a quality to visions, a kind of extreme and detailed clarity, which develops over several days, with the vision becoming more and clearer each day. If a vision comes three times, and evolves in this way, I trust that it is a vision to be implemented, rather than just a fantasy or wishful thinking. I know that it comes from Source and not from my ego.

These three visions fulfilled this pattern, and that told me to pay attention. So then the task was to discern what they meant. What was being suggested to me?

The visions seemed to be presenting me with a need that was asking to be met. They told me that young people in China—university students, in particular—were yearning for more meaning in life. Because of my background, I immediately made the connection to service. Having just retired after creating and then running a Service Learning program for K-16 students in New Mexico, I knew how much meaning flooded into young people's lives when they made a commitment to community service. Still, it was startling to think of this in the context of China, a country with which I was so unfamiliar.

The second vision also told me that that the minority people in China were searching for a way to sustain their traditional culture so that it would not be completely absorbed into the mainstream culture without leaving a trace; they were searching for a way to resist the rush to consumerism that was beginning to grip the country.

To some, the idea of receiving visions may seem quite unusual, even a bit startling, but I had worked for many years on my spiritual practice, so I was very open to receiving guidance from a Source of higher wisdom. In addition, I also had significant experience working with visioning as a very practical tool. My background includes several decades in the corporate business world as an IT manager; I'd also been heavily involved in political campaigns, and served as the executive director of a successful nonprofit. In each of these roles, I'd always been interested in innovation, in discovering ideas, tools, and new perspectives to improve outcomes. As part of my exploration I'd learned how to facilitate others through a visioning process to help them clarify their purpose and goals—whether personal or organizational. Visioning is a universal process, applicable to almost any situation, and I had taken people through this process many times in my work in both the business and nonprofit arenas.

But even with all my experience with visions, the detail and depth of these particular visions stunned me. The content of the visions went beyond my experience. I did not know anything about Chinese minority cultures—or Chinese university students, for that matter. And beyond that, there was the wound I had just sustained. I hesitated, and yet the pull toward the visions was undeniable. *Was I being called to China?*

As I've said, I'd had a strong spiritual practice for many years, and I trust that I will be guided. When the guidance comes, I have opened myself to receive it, and learned to trust it. Because of that trust, I know that I must step into the vision, walk through that opened door. It is not really like having courage exactly, but a special kind of trust in intuition and in the unseen.

That said, I am also a practical person, someone who has successfully navigated the corporate world. I had learned that it was important to test a vision, to see if it was really *mine,* before attempting to carry it out. The way to test a vision is to ask three questions: *May I? Can I? Should I?*

- This first question is about asking permission from Source. To discover this, I posed this question and listened for an answer: *May I attempt to fulfill this vision?*
- The second question is about ascertaining whether we are actually capable of manifesting the vision: *Can I do it? Do I have the skills, time, energy and resources to fulfill this vision?*
- Asking the third question helps clarify whether a vision—inclusive of the tasks involved in fulfilling it—is truly meant for us, given our other obligations. *Should I take this on?* I asked. *Given my life circumstances, should I attempt to manifest this vision, or should it be left to someone else?*

If, when I ask those questions, I sense that the answer to any one of them is "No," then I say "No" to the vision. But if, on the other hand, I get three "Yeses," then I *must* do it.

I got three "Yeses."

The process of asking those three questions verified for me that the visions were genuine, and that I needed to take heed. But the truth is, I already knew. I knew the moment I was given the very first vision that my following it would be the source of my healing. If I were to trust that vision and follow it all the way to China, then I would be healed in the process. And so with my heart pounding I took the next step.

Chapter 2

A New Beginning

. . . If you realize that all things change,
there is nothing you will try to hold on to.

It is a strange thing to be past middle age and to find that one must start over. Little did I know that a whole new life was about to unfold, one that would be so unlike anything I had done before, a life that would blast my heart open in ways I could not have imagined. It is a paradox that very deep heartbreak can also bring amazing blessings. As the Persian poet and mystic, Rumi, once said. “To get the precious pearl you must first smash the shell.” For me, this has been true. I had been really wounded by my partner’s leaving, but the gift in that was that I had nothing left to lose.

It was March of 2005 when my shell was smashed. The loss of my partner had been so difficult that by the end of the year, I didn't think that I could manage Christmas with the rest of my family as we always did; it was just too painful. I was very fragile emotionally, going through a very dark night of the soul. But I had good friends and a deep spiritual practice in the Sufi tradition, both of which helped me get through it.

And all the while, I was asking myself about my future, and something inside me was stirring. If I was going to be in this much pain, I thought, I am going to use it. The idea of going to China to follow a vision was preposterous on the one hand, but eminently sensible on the other. What, after all, did I have to lose? I needed to heal. I was looking for some way to restart my life. Of course, to be completely honest with myself, there was a part of me that just wanted to run away. Later, I could see that in running away from one thing, I was also moving towards another. But at the time, all I wanted was to escape from the memories.

I decided to surrender. I would travel to China to explore my visions, to see if there really was something there I could pour myself into that would be of benefit to young people—and to the minority cultures. I would go there with the clear intention to be of service, but without any fixed agenda, and see what unfolded. I trusted the visions, and I knew that I wanted to follow them. But I did not really know what it all meant or what I would find when I arrived. I just knew that I had to find out. And so I made my decision.

Once the decision was made, I turned my attention to practical matters. It was to be a six-month adventure with no attachment to outcome. I did not want to travel there alone; I felt that would be too challenging. I could not speak the language and was unfamiliar with the culture, but even more than that, I had never traveled alone before. In fact, my whole life to that point had been partnered.

Miraculously, two good friends and their daughter offered to accompany me.

The next order of business was obtaining a one-year visa. In order to do so in those days, one had to be sponsored by an in-country business or NGO (non-profit organization). Habitat for Humanity immediately came to mind. I had worked extensively with Habitat to organize service-learning projects for students in New Mexico, and I'd also supported them personally for many years. I had enormous respect for the work of this organization, so I contacted Habitat to see if they might be willing to sponsor us. In return, the three of us were willing to do whatever volunteer work they might have for us.

And so, another miracle: Habitat said yes! They were currently running projects in China, which involved leading teams of westerners—both adults and international students—to help build homes and other needed structures in rural minority communities, just like those I had seen in my second vision. The synchronicities kept coming. Even more stunning, Habitat's headquarters in China was located in Kunming. Kunming is a large, modern city and the capital of Yunnan Province, which is located in the southwestern part of China. Amazingly, this was the only part of China with which I was even a bit familiar, having traveled there once before. I had liked Kunming very much. Not only that, but Kunming was where Green Lake Park was located—the exact same location shown to me in my first vision!

All this was a sign to me that I was definitely being guided to attempt to manifest the visions. That December, scarcely believing we were actually going on such a speculative venture, we boarded a plane bound for China. When we arrived in Kunming, several members of the Habitat staff were waiting to assist us. They showed us around the city, and helped us find a place to live. The question of where to live was never in doubt for me. When I had been to China before, Kunming was the one place where I had felt totally at home—mostly because of Green Lake Park. Imagine a place where people come together each day to exercise, dance, sing and play music. It is an absolutely captivating place of sound and color, of lush vegetation and serene water. I had never experienced such a sense of community before. It was that park that drew me back to Kunming, and I knew that I had to live near it.

Our living arrangement settled, Habitat showed us how to get around the city and also helped us with buying food and with our banking. Their assistance was an enormous gift. It freed me to begin to explore how to manifest my vision. To accomplish that, I would have to find young people who were longing for meaning in their lives, and then create a project that would enable them to begin to spread their wings. No small order!

I had never lived in another country before, and the prospect of living for six months in China was both daunting and exhilarating. I didn't know the language, I didn't know anyone there and I didn't really know what exactly had drawn me there—except for the visions. The visions showed me WHAT the need was, but they did not tell me HOW I was supposed to go about it; I just saw pictures of me sitting and listening to the young people and the minority people stating their needs. This is how it is with visions, I have found; the end result cannot be forced, and the way to get there cannot be planned in advance. Rather, the way opens as you walk it. I had to simply surrender and trust, trust that I would be guided along the way, that the HOW would unfold over time. Most people are really afraid of acting in this way, without having everything all planned out, and I was no exception. I felt a lot of trepidation. But I also knew that I just needed to take the first steps and the rest would show up.

I was anxious to begin to meet young people, but had no idea how to go about it. The park seemed like a place to start, so I began to spend several hours a day there, just strolling around, listening to the music, or sitting on the bridge. Young people did approach me, seeking to practice conversing in English—this is quite common—but their English was so limited that there couldn't be any depth to the conversation. So, after a little dialogue (in which they almost always asked the same questions, such as: *Where are you from? Are you a teacher?*), they would move on.

Day after day, I continued to go to the park, and day after day, I came back to the apartment disappointed and discouraged. This went on for weeks. I began to fear that nothing more would come of my efforts. Perhaps I had deluded myself, building up the purpose of this trip in my mind, when I was merely trying to escape my inner pain. Even in my morning meditations, I questioned the visions; I allowed doubt to enter.

Should I give up the whole idea and just be a tourist for the next few months?

We had arrived at the Chinese New Year, and soon we found that everything was about to shut down for a week, while people went home to their villages or home cities. On top of that, all of the schools were to be closed for six weeks, so the students I wanted to engage with had all gone home on holiday. At loose ends, my friends and I wandered around Kunming, trying to not get lost, always gravitating toward the park, and wondering what to do with ourselves. It was a very confusing time for us all, but particularly for me, since I had come with a purpose and I was acutely aware that they had come largely to support me. How easy it is to doubt oneself when things do not unfold in the way or in the timing that we expect! I began to wonder idly if we should just tour about, see a bit more of the country, and then go home early. But no matter how strong the doubts, I did not give in to them; I persevered.

And then one day, just when hope was all but fading away, I was given the key that unlocked the door—at least partially. Quite by accident, I met a young family who were originally from Kunming, but now lived in the States. They spoke English, and as we chatted, they told me about an "English Corner" where people gathered to practice their language skills. They told me that it took place in the park one evening each week at about 7 PM. Unfortunately, they didn't know the day or the exact location, but that was enough to give me encouragement. For the next week, I scoured the park each evening at the appointed time, but to no avail. It was so frustrating, and I was again about to give up when, in another chance encounter, I came across someone who told me that the group met on the sidewalk OUTSIDE the park on Thursday evenings.

When Thursday evening arrived, I practically ran all the way to that sidewalk and there, under the streetlights, were about 200 students gathered in small groups, all earnestly speaking English with each other. Scattered here and there, were a few foreigners, each surrounded by much larger groups. I took in the scene, and shook my head. How could I have possibly missed this in all my evenings of looking??? When we get an idea about how something is supposed to be or look, we are often oblivious to anything outside that scope. And so it was with me. I had been looking *inside* the park and so I just didn't see the crowd gathered *outside*. It still amazes me.

And then, all of sudden, I was completely surrounded. A crowd of about 25 students gathered so quickly around me that it astonished me. They were all asking the same questions, the ones I had heard so many times before: “Where are you from?” and “Are you a teacher?” But now there was a new question: “What are you doing here?”

I was excited about that question, because it was an opportunity to talk about coming to China to volunteer, and to encourage others to volunteer. But as I told them about what had drawn me to China, I made a shocking discovery: They had no idea what volunteering was! They simply did not have any concept of what I was talking about. I had to scramble to find a new way to talk about it in a way they could grasp. I found myself speaking about how my life had been so blessed—that I had a good family, a good education, a really good job, and I lived in a beautiful place in a beautiful house—and that now I felt that I wanted to give something back for having received all that.

I finished and looked around. To my great gratification, they were interested. They wanted to know more! As we spoke together, I surveyed their beautiful, inquisitive faces, open and curious, and thought about the vision I'd had of young people searching for meaning. I sensed this might be the start of something.

At the edge of the circle, a young man moved his way towards the center. He had been listening very intently, and I could feel his presence. When he got close enough, he began to ask more detailed questions about what I wanted to do. His English, though full of small mistakes, was sufficient to enable him to speak more deeply than most of the others, so we began an exchange. We talked about NGOs like Habitat for Humanity, about what it feels like when you are serving others and making a difference, and about how it is possible to care for people we are not related to or have never met. We were in our own little bubble, oblivious to all the other young people around us, though they were intently listening, too. There was something about this young man that struck me as extraordinary. His English name was "Will," and I soon asked if he would like to continue the conversation at a coffee shop. We agreed to meet the very next day.

I walked home knowing that something very special had happened. I knew that this young man and I were connected to each other in some inexplicable way. How does it happen that in the middle of a city of six million people, in a country half a world away from where you live, one day you come face to face with someone you suddenly "recognize"?

The next day when Will and I met, I found myself telling him about the visions that had brought me to China, about the feeling that the young people were searching for more meaning in life. He responded by saying that he thought that this was true, that he also felt that way, and that he felt drawn to me and to what I was talking about. He then said that he wanted to help me in whatever way was needed. I was just so completely moved by this young man.

Will then proceeded to tell me all about his life and his family. His English had been very poor, he said, but one day he decided that he wanted to know more of the world, to meet people from other countries, and so he taught himself, pushing beyond what was offered in school. And then, he revealed that his Chinese name meant "Guiding Light." The connection was magical. Four hours passed without either of us having any sense of it, and in the end, we were inextricably linked.

Will and I began meeting every couple of days, brainstorming about what was needed and what we might create. He then introduced me to other students, and again we talked about NGOs, particularly Habitat for Humanity. Then one day, we hatched the idea of pulling together a team of students for one of the Habitat village building trips. This would be groundbreaking, as Habitat had never recruited Chinese volunteers before.

I reached out to my contacts at Habitat, who were receptive, and we scheduled a trip for the summer, a few months hence. Will then began talking to students about going. The die was cast. We were embarking upon a journey together, and we had no clue where it would eventually take us.

In the meantime, I was giving much thought to how to address the fact that Chinese students lacked any concept of volunteering. They had no idea because this, I subsequently learned, was the social norm in Chinese culture; one helped one's family, but beyond that there was no concept of acting on behalf of the greater social good, let alone strangers. I pondered this for a while, and then an idea came to me. What if students had an opportunity to discuss social issues? Wouldn't that naturally awaken a desire to help others? The more I thought about this idea, the more it resonated, but how would I put it into practice? I puzzled over this until, one day, as I was walking past Yunnan University on my way to an expat café, another idea suddenly popped into my head: I should approach the Foreign Language Department there and pitch the idea of starting a discussion group. With an audacity I did not know I possessed, I walked through the door with the intention of doing precisely that. I had never been to the school and knew no one there, but eventually I was directed to the office of the Director of the Foreign Language Department. She spoke good English, and so I sat down with her to explain my idea in a way that I thought would be appealing to her. I told her that I had noticed that the students were quite good at conducting a basic dialog with a foreigner, but that they could not, as yet, “discuss” anything in any real way. To help develop that skill, I offered to run an English discussion group, with of course, a social agenda.

This was a "cold call," and I had no idea how it would be received. I was amazed to hear her saying to me, "You have put your finger on the very limitation of our students. This is a great idea." Then in a kind of small voice she said, "Would you need any money to do this?" I told her "no," and her face lit up. She told me that she would assign two students from the junior class to help, and that they would approach all of the other third-year students about attending. I couldn't believe how easy it had been. There was no red tape, no request for an outline of what I proposed to do, and they were giving us a classroom in which to hold the sessions. We decided on once a week and we were off and running!

Little did I know that this was the birth of an idea that would eventually spread to four other universities, involving many more students that I had yet to meet. Not only that, but many of these students would eventually become a part of teams of volunteers who would do volunteer work in minority villages, just as my visions had shown. But first we needed to plant some seeds.

Chapter 3

What's needed?

Can you love people and lead them
without imposing your will?
Can you deal with the most vital matters
by letting events take their course?

The ostensible purpose of the discussion groups was to provide a forum for improving English conversation, but Will and I also hoped these discussions would raise students' awareness of social issues in China and the world and thus inspire them to consider serving others. We also wanted very much to *empower* the students by encouraging them to think for themselves and providing them with new, useful skills.

As Will and I set about the task of organizing the discussions, we asked ourselves some basic questions, such as: "What will we talk about?" and "How will we run the groups?" We were in total agreement about our goals, but as we expressed our thoughts about how to proceed, it was interesting to discover how we differed in our approaches. Will felt it was important to do everything really, really, well, right from the beginning, so he suggested that I set the structure and topics. I felt it was OK to flounder a bit at first, so long as the students got there eventually, so I resisted the temptation to do that. Wasn't the whole purpose to encourage the students to discover their own strengths?

At this initial stage, however, the students had no idea what to do, so we needed to provide some light structure. Ultimately, we came up with a compromise; we'd begin by asking the students to brainstorm as many potential discussion topics as they could. Once we had a good list, we'd prioritize and whittle it down to the top candidates.

Twelve students had committed to participating in our first discussion group, and they were very excited. For the whole week before the brainstorming session, they spent their nights searching through newspapers and the Internet for interesting topics. I had also suggested that they look for inspiration in their own lives. What were the issues within their families, their schools, their neighborhoods?

With Will's coaching, the students came up with an excellent list, ranging from more personal to global issues. Then, each student was asked to choose a topic that they would then facilitate a group discussion about. This was a completely new idea for the students—they had never done anything remotely like this before—so we created a simple structure to guide them. Will designed a format, suggesting questions they might use to help stimulate or expand the discussion, and I gave them some training in group facilitation skills. I showed them how to ensure that

everyone could participate equally, without any one person dominating, and I also coached them in how to encourage people to deepen their thinking.

With a little light structure in place, the discussion groups began to take off. It was as if they had a life of their own; all Will and I had to do was light a spark.

The discussions were the source of much reflection on my part. I had arrived in China at a time when the prevailing sensibility of the people was one of innocence. Perhaps nowhere was this more pronounced than at the universities. Everyone referred to college students as "girls" and "boys," and they were, in fact, the very pictures of childlike naïveté. The college girls wore Minnie Mouse hairclips, and there was no sophistication at all. The student's thinking was innocent too, honest and pure, and it felt like a breath of fresh air. I found myself thinking that I hadn't experienced anything like this since my youth in the 1950s when TV was just hitting the market and shows like *Leave it to Beaver* and *Howdy Doody* were all the rage. Compared with America, life in China seemed uncomplicated and predictable in the same way it had back then. It was amazing, at the age of 60, to encounter that innocence again, almost like stepping back in time, or walking onto a stage set.

That said, I found both the topics this group of innocents chose to discuss and the ideas they expressed about them fascinating, and I learned so much about the Chinese culture from these discussions. Some of the topics were "safe" but others really "out there," and all of them were very revealing.

Perhaps the discussion that startled me the most was the one about censorship of the Internet. Most of the time, I took part in the conversations, but this time I refrained and just listened. (As a foreigner, I didn't know what repercussions there might be for voicing opinions about such a topic, so I didn't speak, just as I didn't ever discuss politics or criticize the Chinese system of government.) Before the discussion began, I had thought that freedom would be the obvious focus. Wrong. The primacy of freedom turns out to be an American issue. No, the discussion centered on concerns about anarchy. It became clear that all of the students felt that some form of government censorship was necessary in order to keep the country from devolving into chaos. They talked about the fall of the Soviet Union and how that country had sunk to a level of turmoil, giving rise to a flourishing gangster culture, and how the people were suffering because of it. They voiced concern that there were things on the Internet that, if read, could incite riots, and how that would not be a good thing. And they talked about how young children should be protected from pornography. All in all, they opted for censorship.

As I listened, I came to realize how culturally blind I really was. I could not imagine a discussion of this topic in the US ending with anything other than "freedom at all costs," and that would probably have been my position, too. Yet, as I listened, I came to understand how the Chinese students arrived at a totally different conclusion. China has such a huge population, that even I could imagine how frightening the idea of chaos could seem to the people living there. This conversation opened my eyes, and I realized how little knowledge most people in the west actually have about how the Chinese think.

In addition, we had several absorbing discussions about homosexuality and transgender operations. (I was amazed the students even knew about such things as transgender operations). It is a well-known fact that Chinese culture tends to be homophobic, and that there is little tolerance for gays and lesbians in the society. So, much like in the U.S. in 1950s, homosexuality is very hidden. But yet again, my assumptions were blown out of the water. Only one boy expressed the idea that homosexuality was "disgusting;" all the others talked about how research had shown that people do not have a choice about their sexual orientation, that we are born with our brains wired a certain way. Therefore, they felt that society should not shun homosexuals, nor should the government regulate them. They believed one's sexuality to be a private matter, and that homosexuality should be an accepted part of the society.

As for transgender operations, they had no problem with the fact of them at all; rather, the discussion centered on issues of family. What would happen if one's wife or husband changed gender? How would their parents be taken care of, and could the family still stay together? I found the whole conversation fascinating, and I was very proud of them for going beyond their cultural norms and embracing all people.

These discussions also gave me a window into the family structure and dynamics in the Chinese culture. Are you old enough to remember what it was like in the U.S. as the 1950s moved into the 1960s? Parents thought that their kids were crazy and out of control, and they worried about the consequences of things their kids were experimenting with, like drugs and free love. For the young people, the thought of sharing about what you were doing with your parents, or even attempting to have a conversation with them about your beliefs, was inconceivable; the gap was just so huge. This was (and still is) the situation in China between the current generation and their parents.

The students' parents had grown up at a time when the most important thing was security. This focus on security not only influenced what job you took—hopefully, with the government or a stable industry—but also whom you married. Whether you loved a person was considered much less important than his or her future job prospects, what economic level the family was at, whether the two families could get along, etc.

Most of these students were the first in their extended family to go to the university, and many of their families had pooled all of their money so that one of their children—usually the best student—could go. They were then all counting on that one young person to marry a "safe" husband or wife and to get a very good "stable" job so he or she could repay all that money, plus earn more, to provide for their entire extended family. “Stable” usually meant working for the government or one of the government owned industries.

This was a huge responsibility that weighed on many of students. Further, this was not where the new possibilities lay, nor the careers that most attracted the students. They had grown up in a very different world than that of their parents, one infused with western movies, the Internet, and many new types of jobs. They were interested not in security, but in computers and high technology companies, in teaching English at a language school, and in NGO work, work that would bring more meaning to their lives. These were careers that didn't even exist in their parents’ day. In many cases, these were much more lucrative than government jobs, but their parents felt these new kinds of jobs were not secure, and would not enable them to provide for the whole family throughout their lives. This put tremendous pressure on the students, but it was also understandable if you realize there was (and still is) no social safety net in China, no insurance, and no retirement money. So, one had only one's family to rely on.

Further, the two generations' ideas about raising children were different. The students wanted to raise their own children rather than have them raised by their parents, as was the custom. In sum, the new ways were very attractive, but the familial and cultural pressure to continue in the old ways was also very strong, and the students were caught in the middle. For me it meant many afternoons sitting with students, listening and helping them work out in their own minds how to deal with these conflicts. I became a safe and patient listener for them, and I worked hard to help them find a way to bridge the gap.

In a short time, the discussion groups began to catch fire. More and more students became interested, and they spread to other universities in the area. As this was happening, I began to think it might be time to move the conversations into new territory. Through these discussion groups, the students were certainly broadening their knowledge. They had become more and more aware of the social issues within China, and they'd also had the opportunity to hear how young people in other cultures (mostly the U.S. and Western Europe) dealt with similar issues. Now I wanted to see if we might bring the idea of service into the conversation. The way I imagined doing that involved introducing the students to the visioning process I'd used back in the States. In brief, the process involves asking participants to imagine what kind of a world they wanted to live in. After they brainstormed that, I'd ask them to describe current reality. Then we worked on identifying projects that they were passionate about, and that they could actually do, to help close the gap.

I had used this process very successfully with high school kids in the U.S. to help them envision and then create service learning projects, but leading the Chinese students through it presented a new set of challenges. The Chinese educational system is one of very large classes (70 students per classroom) devoted entirely to rote learning. There is one teacher at the front of the room delivering information, which the students are expected to recite back. The teacher tells students what the answers are, and those are the only answers ever considered. Students are never asked what THEY think.

Our students had had a taste of thinking a bit for themselves in the discussion groups, but they were still at the beginning stages. Many had used research to decide the issues and used the prevailing ideas about a topic as their ideas. So when I first asked what projects they might want to work on, there was complete silence in the room. They had never been asked to offer their own ideas before, and they didn't know where to begin.

Now that I understood more about their cultural norms, I could be more patient. So Will and I decided to try again. What kind of world did they want? People have a tendency to put limits on their imaginations, so we told them right up front that they had a magic wand, that they could create any kind of a world they wanted, and that there were no wrong answers.

We asked the question, and then we sat back and waited.

It took patience to sit in silence and just wait for one of the university students to offer something. It took a while, but eventually, someone did. And that was the start. The students began to articulate the kind of world they wanted. Then we worked on describing the status quo. Lastly, we looked at the gap between the vision and current reality and asked: *What's needed?* What could we actually do to help change the current reality to bring it closer to our vision?

Slowly but surely, the students began to respond. They had never before been asked to think in this way, to imagine the world they would actually like to live in, to think about what they might do to help create it. It was intimidating at first, but then we could see that it was exhilarating, liberating.

In time, the students became used to this way of thinking. No, it was more than that; they were on their way to real empowerment. Once put on this path, there was no stopping them. They no longer waited for someone in authority to tell them what to think or do. As we continued teaching this visioning process, they began to awaken to the idea of making a difference, of serving others. I did not know this yet, but in time, many of these students would join together to become volunteer teams. Eventually, because of our training, they would develop the capacity to go into a minority village, understand the needs of the community and design actionable, do-able programs to address those needs. They would even learn how to monitor their results and use that feedback to make corrections and improvements for the future.

They would truly be able to think for themselves.

I had come to China mainly to escape my own personal pain. I really did not know if the visions I'd seen had any real potential. Now, six months later, I knew that they did. As it neared time for me to go back home, I found myself weeping. My work had only just begun, and I knew I had to return.

Chapter 4

A Taste of the Real

. . . A good traveler has no fixed plans
and is not intent on arriving.
. . .Thus the master is available to all people
He is ready to use all situations

Three months later, I arrived back in Kunming on a Thursday afternoon. I had been traveling for a total of 33 hours, and this time, I was alone—but not for long. Will met me at the airport. He knew that I needed to find a new place to live, a place for just one, and he had found me several apartments to look at the moment I got off the plane. I took one immediately and began settling in. To help me, I had a wonderful welcoming committee of three friends, plus my new apartment owner, and two cars (almost unheard of), so that we could all go to pick up my stored items and bring them to my new apartment.

The transition was very paradoxical. On the one hand, I felt somewhat comfortable; I was coming back to a place I knew, where things felt somewhat familiar. But at the same time, the marked contrast between the U.S. and China was delivering shocks to my system. It would take a few days to adjust!

One of the members of my welcoming committee was my friend, Windy, the project director at Habitat for Humanity. I soon learned that she was eager to tell me about an upcoming project. Habitat was about to begin a volunteer build with the Shanghai International School in the village of Ganhaizi, and Habitat wanted me to go along to get a feel for the work.

Ganhaizi, I learned, was situated in the mountains several hours north. It is one of the poorest villages in Wuding County. Most villagers live in structurally unsafe houses that lack any sanitary facilities. Ganhaizi was populated by one of China's many minorities, the Miao people.

Because of my second vision, I had become particularly interested in learning about China's minority cultures—a topic about which I had known essentially nothing before coming here. Now at least I had a basic understanding. I knew that the mainstream culture was Han. The Han are the largest ethnic group in the world, and they constitute approximately 92% of the population of China. But China also has many other ethnic groups, each with their own unique, traditional cultures. By "official" government count, there were 54 different minority groups in China; however, the number was really much higher. As has happened in the United States with Native American tribes, the government has join ed groups together even though they are, in actuality, quite distinct. I was stunned by the diversity in China, as I imagined almost all westerners would be. In-Yunnan alone, there were 26 different minorities represented. I was fascinated by what I had learned so far, and eager to learn more.

I very much wanted to join the Habitat trip, but it was leaving that Saturday afternoon—too soon for me—so we compromised on my joining up with them on Monday.

Bright and early Monday morning I set off, my borrowed backpack on my back, to meet up with a couple of students from Yunnan University (whom I didn't know and who, I was told, didn't speak much English). The Habitat staff had assured me that the students I was meeting would get me to a township near the "build." There, I could meet up with the Habitat van, which would then take me the rest of the way to Ganhaizi. It seemed a bit of a precarious plan, and while walking to meet them, I had the thought that this was a test of pure trust, for I had no back-up plan, and no language skills, if things went awry.

But I needn't have worried; all went smoothly. We met up, and proceeded to the bus station where our journey was to begin. When we arrived, the station was filled to the brim; thousands were trying to get home to families for the mid-autumn festival, which had just started. There were no other foreigners in the crowd, and EVERYONE was staring at me, this stranger in their midst, in wonder and curiosity. It was overwhelming! Yet, after about an hour of standing in line for the tickets, we were on our way.

And what a journey it was, with the city giving way to open fields and rice paddies, and those in turn giving way to small mountains and fertile valleys. It had rained constantly since I had arrived, and this day was no different, with intermittent rain and clouds. But still, it was fascinating to look out over the landscape. We drove through myriad small towns, eventually landing in the township where we were to rendezvous with one of the Habitat staff and the van. The Habitat staffer had come to town to buy food and supplies for the team at Ganhaizi, so I had some time to take in the sights, which involved my standing outside the car and watching the goings on in the street while the car radio blared Chinese pop music. I do not think that anyone in this township had ever seen a foreigner before, because most of the people who passed by stared at me, looking totally shocked!

Errands done, we climbed into the van and were off. In the township, we had acquired two additional passengers, a grandmother with her granddaughter. Both were dressed in traditional Yi minority dress, embroidered jackets with black-and-white pleated printed skirts, and pink plaid wool headscarves tied around their heads. I was somewhat familiar with the Yi people, having seen them in Kunming, but wondered if they would feel uncomfortable with me in close quarters. However, neither seemed to be having any trouble with a foreigner in the car. Grandma kept grinning her toothless grin at me, and the little girl had a bag of candy which she was sharing around the car, not keeping them all to herself as many Western children might do, smiling all the time. So off we went, all squished in the van with supplies jammed in as well, and music blaring on and on.

With one exception, none of the people in the van spoke much English, so I was able to be alone with my impressions. The ascent up to the village was absolutely spectacular, through winding mountain passes and around hairpin curves. Then, as we began our descent, the mountains gave way to valleys with fields of terraced rice and corn. The mid-autumn festival signals harvest time, and so everyone was out in the fields bringing in the rice and corn crops. When I say "everyone," I mean it literally: grandparents, parents, children of all ages, water buffalo, and donkeys with wagons pulled behind. People were walking the mountain roads with unbelievably HUGE loads strapped to their backs, another band around their foreheads to help stabilize the load. The rice crop was spread across the roads so that any vehicle, whether motorized or not, could help thresh it by running over it, and the corn crop was being strung like chili ristras. Thick bunches were hung out to dry under the eaves of every house we passed (though how they dried in all the rain was a mystery to me).

As we approached the town where the Habitat team was staying, we passed a dead cow lying on its back, legs in the air. It was being skinned and butchered by the side of the road. Definitely fresh!!! As for the town itself, there was just one paved road, which ran through the center, continuing on as dirt. There was one guesthouse with a restaurant next door, and a kind of general store selling everything imaginable. Beyond that, there were several cement tables lining the road where people could put out their vegetables, meats and goods for sale, and a few residences. Needless to say our accommodations were basic in the extreme. Our rooms each had four beds made of a plank of wood with a one-inch foam pad, sheet and quilt. There was nothing else in the room, and the one toilet was a "squatter," flushed with water from a bucket.

The next morning we ate our breakfast of hot spicy noodles in a broth along with some fruit that Habitat had brought. We washed it down with tea, and set off. The village where the build was to take place was a half-hour hike up, and then down, a small mountain. As we reached the peak and began our descent down the other side, we could see the village in the distance. It was perched on a small plateau overlooking their cultivated, terraced fields. In the background were absolutely beautiful cascades of mountain ranges, surrounded by mists. At the flat part of the trail was a pine forest, the most vivid emerald green in color. It was gorgeous from a distance, but once we arrived at the village, we were even more stunned by the 360-degree views.

The residents of the village lived in the ancient traditional ways of the Miao minority people, mostly venturing out only as far as the small town where we were staying, or the outlying area just around it. Although they had individual homes, the village people lived communally; they worked the fields together, cooked together in the one kitchen (a small building, with an un-vented fire/cooking area), and ate together on the benches in- and outside the one room schoolhouse. I learned that the school was no longer in service, and that the children now either lived at the school in the town, or made their way there daily by hiking a half-hour hike each way over the mountain, as we had done. In the midst of all this simplicity and tradition, there was one amusing concession to modernity: in front of the school was a cement area with two basketball hoops where the villagers could play.

The Habitat project involved putting up two homes, simple structures, for two of the village families, and so the next day we set to work, digging the foundations. It was actually a rather back-breaking job, involving pick-axing and shoveling/hoeing caliche clay into wheelbarrows and then disposing of it over the cliff ledges.

We began digging the foundation of the first house right in the middle of the village, as daily life went on all around us, just as usual. People came by leading herds of water buffalo and goats. Donkeys loaded down with firewood for cooking passed by, and their cargos were unloaded at the house next door. Wicker panniers filled with newly harvested corn were dumped at another house to be strung into ristras and hung from the roof beams for drying. Sometimes the owner's pigs would wander down onto the digging site, or the roosters, hens and chicks would scurry around. One time, the students were dumping a load of dirt over a ledge only to hear a loud squeal from a baby pig that almost got buried. Boy, can they run fast!

The soon-to-be owners of the new Habitat house worked alongside us all day and every day, barely stopping at all. And during the day, various villagers would stop by and dig with us for a couple of hours, wanting to see their neighbors move into their new home as soon as possible. Everyone laughed and helped each other. By the third day, it began to feel to me as though time was standing still, or even that I had gone backwards in time. All of this seemed to be just as it was in this village hundreds of years ago: very peaceful, incredibly competent, strong and hardworking villagers (men, women, and children) all working side-by-side, with everyone knowing exactly what to do, and just cheerfully doing it. I saw persistence, patience, kindness, cooperation, acceptance, willingness, and ready smiles every day on the part of the villagers.

Meanwhile, the Western students were showing great maturity. Although only high school freshmen, they worked really hard together, rarely complaining about anything. And, when they had free time, they played with the village children.

At one point, as many of us were taking a break, two of the village women whose homes we were building and who worked every day with us, beckoned me to sit with them. One was aged about 50, and the other about 30. The younger one stroked my hair and put her arm around me. They talked and looked at me and smiled as we sat there peacefully together. We were three women who couldn't be from more different worlds, but in that moment we were all the same; all just taking a break from the strenuous work of shoveling heavy clay for 5 hours a day.

At the end of each day, the Habitat team returned to the guesthouse to shower. Since there had not been enough sun to heat the solar water on the roof, our showers were always cold. One day, there were too many people waiting at the main showers, so the Habitat staff directed me to a neighboring house. Jerry, one of the Habitat staff, knew the occupants well and so, while I took my shower, he helped the family prepare the corn for drying. When I was done and it was Windy's turn, I joined him with the grandma and one of the children. Meanwhile, the grandpa chopped up vegetables on the cement for the pigs as mom and other children were beginning to prepare dinner in the attached kitchen area. They included me completely. Then, one of the small kids came out with a coucouple of large cookie-like things, which were shared all around.

There was something so very special about sitting on a very small stool shucking corn with these people, sharing a treat, feeling not at all separate, but part of something that had existed for hundreds of years.

Then, one afternoon in the middle of the week, we all stopped our work and took some time off. We ate lunch together, and played together for the whole afternoon. What an amazing experience it was! Everyone played: children, the Habitat team, parents, elders, women, men. First, the men played a basketball game against the high school boys of the Habitat team and a couple of Habitat staff. The villagers were terrific players and they beat the boys hands down. We even saw the villagers teaching their two-year-olds how to push the basketball around. Then it was decided that the women of the village, dressed in traditional skirts over pants, their wrapped hair held up on top of their heads with a kind of snake-shaped pin, would play the girls. This turned out to be the most fun event of all, since almost none of the women or the girls could play that well, but they put their "all" into it. We all cheered everyone on, villagers and students alike. The women finally won, beating the girls by two points. And then, as if this wasn't enough, we all went out on the basketball court and played duck, duck, goose, red light/green light, and a version of red rover. Everyone. There were 70-year-old elders chasing 4-year-olds around the circle, everyone running as fast as they possibly could.

I learned something about play that day: what a joy it is to just abandon oneself to it completely. At the end, the children all gathered together and sang to us, even the really small kids, led by the older kids, who were maybe 15 years old. It was just so very touching. These kids had almost nothing—just a few donated toys that they all shared, basketballs given to them by one of the previous Habitat teams—and most likely only one set of (very dirty) clothes, which they
were wearing. And yet their faces just shone and they were thrilled to sing to us. The head man of the village played like everyone else, laughing as a small child chased him about. All the adults took care of all of the children and everyone shared everything.

This village was obviously extremely poor in material things. There was no running water, little or no electricity, and the buildings were all in a state of partial collapse, but how very rich this village was in joy! It was truly remarkable. People were always smiling and really happy to see all of us. They joyfully cooked for us and ate with us each noon (though they would not take any food until all the visitors had been served). It made me think that the so-called "civilized" cultures of the world are missing something very, very important.

At the end of the trip, the villagers said that they wanted to sing to us, so they opened up the church that had been built by missionaries, and the villagers came in from the fields. Many were those with whom we had been working all week, people we had seen pick-axing and farming and shoveling. A group of about a dozen, half women and half men, one holding his small daughter, went up front to sing. These are very strong and hardy people, so I fully expected their singing to be rather simple and rough. Yet, when they opened their mouths, out came a glorious four-part harmony, sung with incredible joy, energy and passion. I realized then that these people were genuinely amazing, so totally balanced that they could express all the different aspects of themselves easily. What an inspiration.

Upon my return to Kunming, I found myself contemplating life, and how each of us chooses to live it. Why is a village such as this so enticing to many who live in the West? Is it because life is paired down to only that which is absolutely essential? Are we longing for that? It's as if there is a growing desire in people for a simpler, less complicated life where we're not constantly bombarded by technology, noise and constant stimulation. When you don't have to stay vigilant to manage or block everything that's trying to come in, there's a sense of being very present in the moment.

I had much to think about, and I was glad indeed that I had had a chance to meet the extraordinary people of that little village in the mountains of southwestern China.

Chapter 5

A New Possibility

Open yourself to the Tao,
then trust your natural responses

After my own trip to Ganhaizi, the next step was clear. Excited, I told Habitat that I wanted to organize a team of Chinese students to do a volunteer trip there. To my joy, they agreed.

This was a very important, groundbreaking step in multiple ways. For one, it would be our Chinese students' very first volunteer experience; none of them had ever done anything like this before. It would also be a first for Habitat: the first time they had ever sponsored a volunteer team comprised solely of Chinese citizens. Previous to this, the volunteer teams had been made up of Westerners, either adults or international school students, mostly from the States and Europe.

This trip was also very significant because it represented a first step toward the establishment of civil society in China. The term "civil society" is used to mean when the people themselves assume responsibility for their society and its problems. We in America take this idea for granted. Our country was founded on the idea of “participatory” democracy, meaning that all citizens recognize that they have a responsibility to contribute to the success of the society, not just through economic development, but also through social development. From the very beginning, people knew they had a responsibility to help each other when there was a need. I had seen this in my own life. When I was a child in the 50's, it was a natural part of life to watch out for our neighbors, to shovel snow for the elders or bring meals to those who were sick or grieving. Mothers watched out for ALL the neighborhood children, not just their own. We didn't even think about it; we just naturally did it. I have heard this said by many of my generation.

Yet in China, at least in 2006, this was a concept unheard of in the mainstream culture. We would find out, of course, that this was not true in the minority villages. There, people were very much in the mode of naturally helping others in the same way I had experienced growing up in the U.S. But for the university students this was something radically new. One helped the members of one's family, but beyond that, there was no sense of responsibility for anyone else.

In my view, this cultural norm had robbed them of some very profound emotions of the heart.

Last, but not at all least, this was a very big step for Will. True to the meaning of his name, Will ("Guiding Light") became the first team leader. Will was to organize the trip, selecting the best student volunteers, and then he would lead them as they worked in the village. Will had never done anything like this before, but I had invited him to go with me on one other Habitat volunteer build with a group of international school students, and he watched to see how the leaders worked with the students. Of course, he would not be in charge of the whole trip; Habitat staff would also be there, but I would not be with him; I would be back in the States. So, from that vantage point, he was on his own.

As I expected, Will did an amazing job. He carefully selected 20 students, interviewing each student who wanted to go, seeking out those who had the deepest desire. Many of those chosen were part of a new English discussion group that he had just set up. Confident that he was on the right track, I laid the groundwork for several additional trips to Ganhaizi, and then I left again for America.

These first trips turned out to be an amazing turning point for the students—and for me.

A month later, when I returned to China, a group 21 students from four different universities converged at my apartment. They had all participated in the Habitat for Humanity volunteer team trips that I had helped to set up. They were so excited to see each other again! And then, for several hours, they shared with me about their experiences in Ganhaizi. I was thrilled to hear how much inspiration they had drawn from our training and discussions about service. For example, they told us how, at the end of each day at dinner, they did a "sharing," during which they each told the person on either side of them how much they appreciated them. Then they told me how, on the last day, when the team was breaking up, they had all cried at the loss, even the male students, as one of the young women told me. Many talked about what they wanted to do for their *next* volunteer experience, and about how they were sharing their experiences with their friends and family.

As I listened, my heart overflowed. It was so incredibly moving to hear how grateful they all were for the opportunity to volunteer. Only a year ago, these students hadn't had any idea what volunteering is, or what a nonprofit organization is. Yet on that day, they were talking about how important volunteering is to having a more meaningful life!

Over the next weeks, more opportunities for volunteering began appearing. The following week, for example, we organized another student volunteer team to work at a children's center run by Save The Children UK, assisting their anti-child trafficking program participants. Our students would teach two classes, one in computers and one in English. If successful, the program would expand to art and dance programs. One of the students who participated in that project took the time to reflect upon her experience in a letter to me:

I want to express my gratitude to you for the very good you did to the voluntary project. I can touch your kindness and caring to the countryside in China. It is a great inspiration for me to take actions to do what is within my ability to have a change. I learned more about the student volunteering. I learned when I have an idea I shouldn't worry about my capacity. I shouldn't worry about what other people will think about my action. I shouldn't worry about something financially. The one thing and the most important thing I should do is taking actions. Besides I also experienced how powerful it is when several people who own the same idea, go on their way together according to the direction their idea has given them.

Something was happening to the students! Their hearts were opening to something beyond just themselves and their families. This was that first vision, come true in reality, and I was filled with gratitude. And, as the programs began to expand to other villages, I began to think more about those people whom the students touched, the minority people. Was the second vision about to unfold as well?

With all this possibility on the horizon, I no longer had any doubts. I knew, now, why I had come to China.

Chapter 6

Laying Fear To Rest

She who is centered in the Tao
can go where she wishes, without danger.
She perceives the universal harmony,
even amid great pain,
because she has found peace in her heart.

One morning the phone rang. It was Windy from Habitat for Humanity calling to tell me that the head office was sending a photographer to do a feature story on Habitat's work in leprosy villages in China. They were traveling to some of these villages the next day. Did I want to join them?

A leprosy village? I quickly searched my memory for what I knew about leprosy. I remembered reading about it in medieval mystery stories, a disease so horrible that the victims were shunned and sent away from their families to live in leper colonies. And, to the best of my recollection, I had also read that it was very contagious!

Beyond that, I knew very little. I had never met anyone with leprosy before, and I found myself feeling afraid. Yet, even as I felt trepidation, I knew I wanted very much to go. Fear often stops us from experiencing life fully, but I wasn't going to let it. That was my commitment to myself. So I took a deep breath and said, "Yes."

Habitat had hired a car and driver to take us to Yangbi, a town in northwestern Yunnan province. From there, someone from the local government would chaperone us to the village. Yangbi sits on the other side of the mountain from Dali, a famous walled city that is a very popular tourist attraction. I had never been to the other side of the mountain, and was interested to see a new area. Plus, Yangbi is known for its walnuts (very yummy), and for the creations the local artisans make from the nut's inner structure and shells: amazing things, like tables and lamps, bowls, and objects d'art. I was looking forward to seeing them.

Once we arrived in Yangbi, we were taken around to sightsee, visiting several shops where I could admire the local crafts. Eventually, we ended up at the government health office in town. Thus began the waiting and the endless rounds of tea with government officials. This custom was one of the most challenging things I experienced in China because the conversation was always all in Chinese (of course). If I listened very hard I could pick out a word here and there, but after about 15 minutes, I could no longer sustain my attention. Much of this tea and talk involved endless posturing and proffering about "who you know," so I was generally very glad that I didn't have to listen to it.

Eventually, we were taken outside and led to a shiny, new four-wheel-drive government car. Behind the wheel sat a Chinese soldier in full uniform. I had not been in China very long, and this was my first encounter with the military—a bit intimidating to a foreigner. Before this thought could fully register, Windy, the photographer, and I were quickly bundled into the back seat, with the driver and a doctor from the health department in the front. Thus began one of the most bizarre car rides I have ever taken.

The road to the leper village was rough in the extreme, more like a boulder-strewn cart track, really, so we were being tossed around fairly badly. I was starting to question my decision when, about a third of the way through the journey, the driver did something totally unexpected. He rummaged around in his bag and suddenly pulled out a CD. which he then slipped into the car's player. And what did he play? American oldies! Here I was, a sixty-something American woman, sitting amidst a carload of Chinese people—one of them a government soldier—all of them talking Chinese a mile a minute, tucked away in a remote corner of China, on our way to a leprosy village, and what was I doing? Singing along with "oldies but goodies," all of which I knew by heart. What was the chance of that happening? In that moment, I saw that it was true: when we refuse to let fear stop us and take a risk, things can happen that we might never have imagined possible, not in a million years.

That particular moment will always stand out because it was so rich and full and unexpected. And so was the rest of our journey. In another surprising twist, the driver occasionally stopped to point out native healing herbs and flowering shrubs, interested to know if we had them in the U.S. So much for my assumptions!

Three hours later, we finally arrived at the village. Many residents came out to greet us, happy to have visitors because they were so rare. As we were escorted about, we were shown what Habitat had recently built for them. It was a long row of one-room dwellings. Each had cement floors, a single door and one window for light. There was room for only a bed, a table and a small fire ring for cooking. It was the most basic of basic accommodations, and I found myself questioning why Habitat had decided to build something so crude—until I saw the old building this had replaced. It was a string of medieval hovels, each dirt floored, with only a door, and no window. The straw mats on the floor were falling apart, and the roof was half falling in; they were uninhabitable by any standard.

As we were inspecting the rooms of this old building, we came upon one that was still being inhabited. A very old man lay on the mattress on the floor. He looked up at us and smiled the sweetest smile you could imagine. With that, my heart swelled open. This man was in one of the worst situations a human being could ever find himself, and yet he smiled.

Later, we asked why the old man was still living in the old building, and we were told that the change to a new living space would have just been too much for him. He had lived much of his life in that hovel, and it was home.

That evening, we went back around the mountain to Dali. We spent the night there, and the next day traveled on to a second leper village. This village was not at all as remote as the first, but it had rained quite a bit over the previous days, so the track from the main road to the enclave was impassable by car. We piled out, leaving the driver down below, and headed up the low mountain on foot. It was a challenging hike, but an hour later, our feet covered in mud, we were walking the last bit through a lovely orchard into the village. The villagers had been told we were coming, so they had been waiting patiently. When they finally saw us, the entire population came out to greet us. We were swarmed, and the village was transformed into a sea of smiles and laughter.

The photographer had been to that village before, the previous year, so it was a reunion of sorts, and there were many claps on the back for him. He wanted to set to work immediately, and the villagers responded like a bunch of kids, all wanting to be in the pictures, hamming it up.

After the first group had been photographed, they headed off back to the fields to work. Even though many of these people had lost parts of their bodies, they still had to do their part to support the whole. I stood by and watched them go. Some were climbing up the hill on crutches; still others had made adaptations to the hoes for their fingerless hands. The sight was very moving and inspiring.

As the photographer continued with his task, Windy and I explored the village. Both of us loved handmade baskets, so we searched for the village basket maker. What we found was a man in his mid-sixties who had lost both his hands. Having only stumps at the wrist, I could not imagine how he could possibly make a basket, and yet he seemed to make ALL the village baskets.

We sat and watched him for quite a while. He had devised an ingenious technique: having attached a leather pad to his wrist, he used it to push a tool that would, in turn, draw the bamboo through the lattice framework. The end results were beautiful. I managed to buy a few of his older baskets as well as a small wooden stool he had made. They decorate my home to this day, and each time I see them, I think of him.

As the day wore on, we realized that we had had nothing to eat since breakfast, and it was nearing 3 pm. We did not want to ask the villagers for any food, concerned that we might deplete their small food stores.

One of the villagers must have been psychic though, because no more than 15 minutes after we realized how hungry we were, she arrived with boiled eggs, two for each of us. Once again, I experienced the extreme generosity of those who seemed to have the least. In that moment, I wished that all the people in America could be here to bear witness to this. Many Americans have much more than we need, and yet many of us share nothing at all. We have much to learn from these villagers.

When it was time to leave, I realized how grateful I was that I had not listened to my fears, for these villagers had touched me deeply. These people had suffered so much, yet they refused to let life's hardships stifle their playfulness and joy. It had been such a privilege to meet them.

There were many lessons here for me, and much inspiration. I was still in a great deal of pain because of what had happened to my marriage. My heart still felt like it had been ripped open, and I was sometimes overcome by loneliness. But even though I was still raw, I could feel how much harmony there was in these humble villages, especially here, in a leper colony. An unforgiving disease had shattered these people's lives. Then they'd been exiled from society, pushed away from everything and everyone they'd ever known and loved. Yet, they were smiling and welcoming to strangers!

Through these strong, simple people, I was re-discovering something I had nearly forgotten: that the world is a beautiful place. Beyond whatever pain, suffering or trauma any of us may experience, there is an underlying grace and beauty to life, just as the Tao says.

Chapter 7

Stepping Forward

The Master allows things to happen.
She steps out of the way
and lets the Tao speak for itself.

Time seemed to be passing so quickly, and before I knew it, it was time for Will to graduate from college. Our collaboration had been so rich and fulfilling for both of us, that I asked him to spend the next year working with me, in partnership, to expand the program. To my great relief and joy, he agreed. So we set to work.

By then, it had become clear to both of us, that in order to keep this idea alive, we needed to create some sort of organizational structure. Rather than just opting for the usual top-down pyramidal structure, we wanted to approach this thoughtfully and creatively, so we developed a list of criteria. Our structure needed to be flexible enough to be sustainable, in the sense that it needed to take into account the fact that students DID graduate and move on, and that new students would always need to be recruited to fill the jobs.

I also very much wanted this to be a collaborative effort, so we needed to create a structure that would foster that as well. I believed that collaboration was essential; previous experience had taught me that. Back when I was in my 20s, working in business and also volunteering for political organizations, I had operated in a very adversarial way. And I was good at it, really good at it! I knew how to garner support for my side of an issue, and win. But over time, I realized the failings of that win-lose approach. I was involved with the political process long enough to see the unanticipated consequences; I saw the same issues coming back around again and again. When the losing side got back into power, they almost inevitably wanted to go back to and overturn the issue the other side had just fought for and won. That's because the win-lose approach-never really resolves anything. So I'd come to see firsthand that win-win is the only thing that really works. And true win-win only comes about by working together to create a shared vision.

Creating a shared vision is also essential because the whole really is greater than the sum of the parts. As an individual, my thinking is limited; but if you and I think *together,* we can think much bigger than either of us separately.

And so, a structure that was sustainable, collaborative and could facilitate shared vision was born. A group of five students came together to form a kind of central organizing team, with each in charge of a specific project. In addition, Will and I worked in partnership to consider the larger needs of the organization. We were all equals, with each having a voice in the major decisions. Because my focus had always been on empowering the students, I was careful not to lead them too much. Rather, to make sure they benefited from my experience, I would gently suggest things or ask questions that might prompt their thinking, and then back off to give them the space to come up with their own ideas or solutions.

It was in that spirit that Will put forth an idea. He suggested that we needed our own office, a place where students could gather and we could hold meetings. Up to that point, we had been using classrooms loaned to us by Will's university, but things were definitely evolving—more and more students from different universities were interested in participating, and we were becoming a force on our own—so that option was no longer adequate. We needed a place that was more centralized, and not attached to any one campus.

I agreed, and so Will went off to look. In short order, he found office space in an older Kunming neighborhood. It was nearby all the universities, which was great, and the rent was cheap, which was also great. But the rent was so reasonable because it was also quite run down; in fact, it was really grimy. That was a problem that could be easily solved, though, and again the solution came from the students. They decided to paint it to make it look more "professional," as they put it. That's when the magic started to happen.

After the students finished painting the office, they stood back and assessed the result of their efforts. The office had been transformed into a very attractive and inviting space, and they were thrilled. Then they looked around and saw that the corridor leading up to the office was dirty and dark and not very hospitable. They decided to paint the walls in the entryway so that the whole environment would be light and bright, and welcoming for all those coming in.

Once that was completed, the students thought their job was done. It turned out, however, to be only the beginning, for one by one, the residents of the building started showing up at the office door, asking whether the stairwell might also be painted so that they might enjoy a bright, clean way up to their apartments.

The students decided to oblige.

As the students painted their way up the stairs, they got to know the residents of the building. Most were elderly and impoverished. Many had been essentially abandoned, both by their children and the city, and they felt that no one cared about them. But by the end of the month, the stairway to all seven floors of the building had been scrubbed clean and painted a bright white, and the residents were ecstatic. Because of the actions of the students, they began to feel that they were NOT just abandoned, that someone DID care about them.

Then, as the weeks went by, people in the neighborhood began to notice the change in this building, and they, too, came to the door knocking, asking if their buildings might be painted, too.

Thus, the Light Community program was born. Light Community was our first student-created program. Up to this point, the students had been volunteering on projects organized by international organizations like Habitat for Humanity. Never before had they stepped out to create something on their own. This was a huge leap forward.

All along, I had been endeavoring to inspire and empower the student leadership team. I was always telling them that they could create whatever projects they could imagine, that they only needed to see what was needed. When I first began to say this, however, all I got back were blank stares. The students just didn't understand. They didn't have a clue as to what was needed, really; in fact, they didn't even know how to think in this way. They had been raised to do what they were told, to follow the directives of their teachers and family members. Students would acquire large amounts of complex information, but they were never asked what THEY thought. They were never encouraged to think for themselves, and they were certainly never encouraged to create anything. This is a huge deficit in the educational system of China.

And then, suddenly, here was this woman from the United States, a bit culturally ignorant at that time, blithely saying, "You can do ANYTHING that inspires you and is needed. Well, what do you want to create?" Of course they gave me blank stares! But then there they were, suddenly being asked to paint all of these stairwells, and something miraculous began to happen. They *did* begin to see for themselves what was needed, and they rose to the occasion and created this new Light Community program.

Organizationally, Light Community was perfect for us; it provided an ongoing stream of manageable projects that student teams could work on during the weekends, without extensive travel outside the city. The Light community program became a tremendous success. Teams of 15-20 students painted stairwells in the community every other Saturday for two years. By the end of that time, we'd painted all 7 floors of 22 houses in the community, with about 250 students from several universities participating.

In the process, we came up with a name for our fledgling organization. The students decided to name it *EXiDEA*, which to them meant "excellent," "exceptional," and "exchange of ideas."

Chapter 8

We Are Always Unfolding

. . The Master gives himself up
To whatever the moment brings.
. . . He doesn't think of his actions;
They flow from the core of his being.

The students had been growing tremendously—and so was I, right alongside them. When I first arrived in China, I had known virtually nothing about this country and its culture. Yes, I had traveled a lot throughout the world, but I had never lived in another country for more than five weeks. And yes, I had been to Japan many times, so I thought I had some notion of Asian cultures, that they were alike in some ways. But I couldn't have been more wrong.

When I first arrived, everything was new and exciting, just as it feels when one is taking a three-week vacation in a new place, like Italy or Australia or Mozambique. I had done just that in all three of those places, so at first I drew upon that experience. "Oh, this feeling is familiar," I thought. "I'm not in such a strange place after all." But as time went on, and those first weeks turned into a month and then several months, things became harder, while at the same time, more routine. I began to miss my friends and family, and there were many things I did not understand or know how to do. Add to this the fact that I could not communicate verbally with anyone who didn't speak English—which was most everyone I met on a daily basis. Then consider the fact that I could not read *anything*—not a street sign nor a shop name, nor a newspaper or book. It is amazing how much knowledge of European languages one acquires via osmosis over the years. Whenever I traveled to those countries, I never felt completely at a loss. Even if I wasn't fluent in the language, I could decipher menus, street signs, or look things up in a phrase book. But none of this worked in China. None.

For the first time in my life since I was a toddler, I was functionally illiterate.

It was a really strange thing to be illiterate in a culture that was so overwhelmingly massive and also so alien to me. I did not have any sense of being able to participate in things, nor did I have any idea about what was happening in a given moment. I could not go many places without having a Chinese speaker with me, nor could I manage any of my daily affairs alone. This was all very new to me, and I soon discovered that things that might be tolerable for short periods of time become increasingly difficult as time wears on.

Back home, I was independent and highly competent, but here, I was reliant on others, which began to make me feel very, very vulnerable. The sense of helplessness one can feel in a foreign country was driven home one evening during my first few months in China. I was alone in my apartment, when I realized that I had a case of food poisoning. I'd gone out to have something to eat at one of the local restaurants and then returned home. Soon, it became apparent that things were not right in the tummy and I became violently sick. I collapsed in bed, unable to do much of anything for myself.

I knew I was in trouble. I would need medicine and fluid, as I could already sense that I was dehydrated. I knew I should call someone, but whom? My only friends were in Vietnam. They'd left on a kind of vacation, but I had stayed behind because things had just begun to move with the student program and I didn't want to leave it. Anyway, my phone was in my purse in another part of the apartment, and I didn't have the strength to go get it.

I lay there in the dark, feeling really scared, realizing just how alone I was, and that I could not communicate with anyone. And then I heard something, and realized that my computer had been left on. Suddenly, I saw there was a message from Will asking me how I was doing. Summoning all my strength, I managed to reach the keyboard and wrote back, telling him how sick I was. At that time, we had only known each other for a couple of months, and he was only a junior in college, but somehow I thought he might know what to do. His response was: "I will be there in 10 minutes." This young man never hesitated for a moment, and all I could do was cry. He arrived, as promised, in just a few minutes, bringing with him medicine, rehydration salts and rice gruel (which is what the Chinese give their sick children).

Will stayed by my bedside long into the night, dozing in a chair, until he was sure that I was beginning to feel better, and then returned the next day to check on me. I could never have imagined being so well cared for in such a circumstance in a foreign country. From that day forward, I never again worried about my wellbeing during my time in China, and my trust was rewarded. There would be other times when I got sick with one thing or another. Each time, students or friends would take care of me. During those moments I felt very loved.

The lack of language continued to challenge me, yet I knew I had come to China with an open heart, the ability to be intuitive, and a belief that these things would see me through. I had been in foreign countries before, surrounded by people who were not speaking my language and so I knew that I could communicate quite a lot with my eyes, through gestures and pointing—and through my heart. In one of my earliest communications back to my family and friends, I wrote of my experiences of this.

Imagine a dawn coming late, after 7 AM, and the sky is just lightening in the east. The air has a chill to it but the sky is clear and promises a warm late spring day in a few hours. I have gotten up to go to find the tai chi class in the park. It begins at 8 AM. My apartment is only one street from the beginning of the park and I have to go down six flights of stairs from the apartment and another long flight to the street level, so I use the stairs to begin my warm-up process.

There has been some rain over the past few days, so the air is moist. As I enter the park, there are mists rising over the lake shrouding everything in a gauzy sort of vision-you are able to see shapes moving through it, but it is not distinct. I have become familiar with the layout of the park, so I know where I am going—I've been told of a specific group that a friend's husband goes to.

This is my first time in the park in the early morning. People are exercising everywhere individually and in groups. I pass three other tai chi classes before I make my way to the one I am after, and through the mists, I see a group of people warming up. They all look very hard at me and then smile saying "Nihou," or "Hello." They all begin to beckon me to join them and give me the place just behind and to the right of the teacher so that I can watch him closely. I feel so included. There is no exclusivity at all with the people here.

Tai chi is really hard to do, and even the simplest of moves take a great deal of focus, but it is also incredibly grounding and fluid at the same time. I have now gone to this class for five mornings, and each morning I am greeted like a friend and member of the group. I am beginning to feel the movements in my body, as one does as one learns to dance. Something begins to take over in you. The teacher and some of the really good members of the class have taken time each day to teach me separately so that I can learn the more subtle nature of each move.

I love this place and the people here. There is something so real, kind and genuine about them.

Through my frequent sojourns in the park, I had begun to get to know people, and little by little, I was beginning to feel as though I belonged. One Sunday, I spent several hours dancing in the park. The next day, I went back. I had no idea if there would even be any dancing, since we'd danced for several hours the previous day, but to my joy, the group was there again. One of the female dancers spoke pretty good English, and she wooed me into the circle beside her.

The woman who was leading the dancing intrigued me. I could tell from her clothes that she was from a minority group that lived somewhere south of here, near the Vietnam border. After I had been dancing for a while, she came over to tell me that I was a very good dancer. Grinning, she took my hand, indicating that I should dance next to her. The group all got such a kick out of my participating and doing well. Many people nodded to me and gave me a thumbs-up as I left to return home.

As I walked, I reflected. On the way out the door that afternoon, I had bumped into the owner of the Italian restaurant in the neighborhood, and we talked for a few minutes on the sidewalk. Then, while I was coming back into the building, I bumped into one of my neighbors, a Belgian. By now I also knew and greeted most of the young girls who "womanned" the concession booths in the park. They usually waved at me and I said "Nihou" to them. That day, several other people I'd danced with the week before recognized me and beckoned me to come into their circle also. I was beginning to be recognized, beginning to make a life here.

Then, while walking back across the park, I bumped into Angela, a woman I had met only briefly. She was a member of the Naxi minority.

The Naxi people live in the vicinity of Lijiang, about seven hours to the north of here, close to Tibet and in the middle of very high mountains with snow on them year round. I learned from a guidebook that the Naxi people have Tibetan roots, and she looks quite Tibetan. I spontaneously invited her to join me and a friend for dinner. She accepted, and brought us a video about her ethnic minority. She also brought over her traditional clothing, which she put on my friend's daughter (and later, me). She was wearing another type of their more everyday clothes, and we took pictures of all of us dressed up together.

We all had so much fun together, laughing a lot. Angela sang her native songs along with the video in an astoundingly beautiful voice. She said that her people sing all the time and everyone in the village has a beautiful voice. One part of the video showed two young people courting; they do it by singing about love to each other. Wow, the west is certainly missing the boat in many ways!

Angela then told us that her niece, Jess, was due to have a baby in five weeks, and I immediately wanted to make her a baby quilt. Without a machine, I would need to sew it completely by hand, but I was looking forward to making my first quilt for China.

Jess Yang

Then, one day, during my first year in Kunming, I was in the park watching a group of singers, musicians, and dancers performing. I noticed one of the women dancers especially, for she had the most amazing eyes. She was also incredibly alive, and I found I couldn't take my gaze away from her. As I was watching, she noticed this in me, and began gesturing for me to join her in the circle. I was embarrassed, and a bit afraid. For one thing, there were about 100 people watching, and I did not know how to do the dance she was doing. Plus, I was the only foreigner there, so I knew I would be quite a spectacle.

I said no, but she kept insist ing, trying to get me into the circle, and I kept shaking my head and refusing. But then, in that moment, I had a strange, new thought: "No one knows me here. I will most likely never even meet any of these people again. It is OK to make an ass of myself in public."

Always before, whenever anything like this presented itself, I had stopped myself. But now it was time to let go. So I entered the circle and did my best to imitate what she was doing. I concentrated on that, and on her eyes, which were full of mischief and life, rather than on all the people who were staring at me (and yes, they were staring!). Eventually, she even invited me to dance a waltz with her, with the musicians playing along. It was an enchanted moment. I had never experienced anything like it.

I left the park that day feeling exhilarated. I knew that, because of this, there was now more of "me" available to both others and myself.

For two whole years after that, I looked and looked for this woman almost every day as I walked through the park, but I never saw her again. I often wondered about her. As the memory grew fainter, I began to wonder: had she been a mirage? Then, one day, toward the end of 2008, I was walking through the park to one of the cafes on the "Western" street with one of my student friends, when I happened to glance over at a group gathered around a dancer. And there she was. I couldn't believe it! She saw me at almost the same moment and came running over, throwing her arms around me. It felt like we were long lost friends meeting up again after a long absence. I sat with her for a while, and my student friend, Ma Jing Jing, translated for us. It turned out that she had gotten sick and was just coming back to the park

after a two-year absence. She was about my age; I think maybe one year older. Then, after finally finding out more about each other, we danced once again in complete joy at having found each other. I consider her one of my closest friends, even though we have no way of communicating with each other—except through our hearts.

And there are other ways in which I was changing, not the least of which was my physical body. I had lived many years in downtown Boston before moving to Santa Fe. I was a young woman then and walked every day to work, to dinner, and to go shopping, which enabled me to stay thin and fit. But when, in my 40's, I moved to Santa Fe, I found that I had to travel mostly by car to get even the most basic of my daily tasks done. Though I did hike quite a lot in the mountains, it was not the same kind of daily, consistent exercise that I had been used to, so I'd found myself becoming physically lazier and weaker. Now here I was, back in a big city and having to walk everywhere—often several miles a day. Even better was the fact that I lived on the 6th floor of my building and so I had to go up and down those stairs several times a day. Add to this, tai chi in the morning and dancing several times a week, and I had become one active lady. In fact, I could often "out walk" or "out work" most of the university students.

That all sounds good for my health, I know, but there was also a much deeper, more profound shift taking place in me: my sense of self had changed. Although I had always been a relatively strong person, over the years, due to aging and then being left for a younger woman, my sense of my abilities—and of my very self—had been diminished. But being in China alone, being successful with the student program, and then bringing my body back into good shape changed all that.

I had found myself again, in an entirely new way, and it had opened me up once again to a sense of infinite possibilities.

Chapter 9

Deep Loss

Seeing into darkness is clarity.
Knowing how to yield is strength.

A great Sufi mystic, Abd Abdul Jilani, once wrote in one of his discourses that God will smash your heart open and then will lovingly care for you, and then He will smash your heart open again and lovingly care for you, and then. . . God had smashed open my heart when my partner of many years left me for another woman, and He had certainly lovingly cared for me over the next years as I healed.

And then my heart was smashed open again.

Will and I had worked closely together for three years creating EXiDEA. We'd traveled together as well and shared deeply from our hearts, telling each other about ourselves, our dreams, our lives. One time, after about two years of our working closely together, I confided in him that I missed being hugged, for the Chinese culture does not touch. Will responded by putting those customs aside, and giving me the hug I so sorely needed. Will, I knew, was a special person, not only incredibly bright but also kind and thoughtful as well as visionary. By now, he had been out of college for a year, and I knew it would soon be necessary for him to make some decisions about his future for, although I was paying him a small salary, I knew he could not stay. I'd put this out of my mind to focus on the work, but then, one day, the inevitable happened: he came to me and told me that he had a job offer to work as a translator for a very large Chinese construction company. The job would be very challenging, and it would require him to re-locate to Sri Lanka, but it paid four or five times more than the average salary for someone just a year out of college. It was an opportunity that just had to be considered.

During our many conversations, Will had told me about his childhood, and especially about his mother, about how determined she had been that Will receive a good education. She had been working at a business she loved, but when she realized that the school he was attending was not very good, she gave up her job and moved the family to another city where the schools were better. Will loved his mother dearly, and recognized what a huge sacrifice she had made for him. He was also acutely aware of what was expected of him. In the Chinese culture, once a young man marries, he is not only responsible for the wellbeing of his wife and child, but also for the wellbeing of both his own family of origin and his wife's. Sometimes this obligation also included their extended family. It was a HUGE responsibility, and it put great stress on the young people burdened with it.

Will's family was not pressuring him, but his younger sister was not doing well in school, and his mother was struggling to make ends meet. In considering his next step, he told me that he realized that he was facing a choice between doing what duty was asking him to do, and what his heart wanted. He said that he loved the work that we were doing together, but that he knew that he would need to take the job and leave China.

Of course, I understood his decision completely. And, at the same time, I was devastated. Will and I were very close and deeply connected.

He had become my best friend in China, and we shared a common vision. So, despite my rational understanding of the situation, I felt my heart smashed once more, and I plunged into another dark night of the soul. This situation was nowhere near as traumatic as what had happened with my husband, of course, but it was still distressing. I felt the wind go out of my sails, and I wondered whether I could continue the work without Will as a partner, or even if I wanted to.

Will, ever responsible, found someone to replace him at EXiDEA, but I found that I could not easily work with this new person. I felt no connection to him. With Will, the creation process had been both shared and effortless, but with the young man who succeeded him, it was work. After a short while, I didn't see how it could go on. I felt terribly torn. I felt called to continue; the work with the students was very fulfilling, and it had already opened many, many hearts, but my own heart was breaking once again.

I decided to keep going. Unable to work with Will's successor, I decided to go back to working with the five-person student team, but without a partner. Then, in time, a new leader began to emerge. Jenny (Chen Xue) was in her third year at the same university that Will had attended. She and I began to work more closely together, and I found that she possessed some important leadership skills. They were different from Will's, but they seemed to be exactly what EXiDEA needed at the time. Not only that, but she was giving me the sense of partnership that I needed to keep going. Then, after about six months, Jenny said that she would be willing to take on Will's job. Jenny had wonderful people skills, and she had many ideas about how to make the program better, how to strengthen the student teams, and how to build the EXiDEA community by keeping in touch with former volunteers after they graduated. It was Jenny who kept the program going, and Jenny who dragged me out of the darkness I had fallen into with Will's departure.

Jenny (ChenXue)

Chapter 10

A Giant Leap Forward

. . . The master has no possessions.
The more he does for others, the happier he is.

For several years now, we had been working with Habitat for Humanity. To date, we had organized and sent three teams of university students on Habitat building projects, and I could only imagine the work expanding. Then came another blow. Habitat China decided that each student who wanted to participate in a build would have to make a substantial contribution to the organization. This was in addition to covering the costs associated with their trip. This additional expense just was not possible for most of our students, and so, with heavy hearts, we thought we would have to cancel the two trips planned for that coming summer, disappointing about 50 students.

But then we looked at the obstacle that had been put in our way—and we decided to go around it. We realized that we did not necessarily need to go through Habitat to organize a volunteer trip; we could organize *our own* trip. So we began to look for a village to work with.

I was due to return to the States soon, but before I left China, I went with students to several villages to do some reconnaissance. Our hopes were high, but for one reason or another, none were suitable. As I departed, the students promised that they would keep looking, and sure enough, they did. I had left in June, and at the beginning of July, I received a phone call from them telling me that they had found a suitable village just a few hours south of Kunming. I was thrilled, and asked them if they felt they wanted to go ahead and organize a first trip. They answered "yes," and within three weeks, the student leaders had not only managed to plan a trip, but had actually led one, bringing the first team of students to the village! The logistics they handled were not insignificant: they had negotiated with the village to come up with a suitable project, and then arranged for buses and housing for the volunteers. They had also organized the villagers to help with the build and to cook meals for the volunteers. They also helped the villagers to purchase the necessary materials.

I was unbelievably impressed with their accomplishment, for none of them had done anything like this before; it was confirmation of my deep belief in the empowerment approach I had been using. Not only had they conducted a successful trip, but from their descriptions, the experience in the village sounded extraordinary. A second trip was now in the works, and nothing could keep me away. I needed to be there to meet these incredible villagers and to watch the team in action. I changed my tickets and returned to China early.

The village was in Tonghai County, in the southern half of the province. It was actually one of several sub-villages that made up one larger village. There were about 200 people in this sub-village, all from the Yi minority, a minority that had its own language and culture of ceremony, music, dance, and folk art. It was also a village where none of the residents had ever met a foreigner before, so I was unsure of the welcome I would receive.

We left Kunming at 8 AM Monday morning, and as we rode on the bus, the students practiced some songs that they wanted to sing to the villagers in gratitude on the last day of the trip. There was much excitement and enthusiasm as different groups of students took turns practicing the two songs. I managed to learn one of them myself, even though it was in Chinese; it was about friendship. Then they all played the kinds of games we used to play in the car on the way to summer camp. In this case, it was boys against girls. The girls won every time!!

The village lay at the end of a very winding, switchback road that led up into the mountains, through thick pine forests, eventually giving way to a stunningly beautiful view. Distance-wise, the village was located only about a 30-minute drive from the closest town, but because of its seclusion, it seemed completely remote. Perhaps this was what gave it a special quality, something that I began to sense immediately. As we entered the village square, we passed by a group of men standing around a squealing pig, and soon discovered that they were in the process of slaughtering that pig and another. It turned out that one of the elderly grandmothers had died that day and the pigs were being killed for a funeral feast that would be attended by about 300 people from this sub-village and all those surrounding ones as well. It was an abrupt, but very real beginning to our visit. You know where your food comes from in this village, whether it was

vegetables, pork, or chicken; the process of slaying these animals was not hidden at all.

As our small vans arrived in the square, villagers began to gather to greet us. It was amazing to experience how enthusiastically they welcomed us, and how open they were, eager for us to become part of their community. Many invited us into their homes to meet and visit with them. In the midst of our welcome, rain began to fall, lightly at first, and then quite heavily, and the time for those visits became now. As we ran for the houses, the villagers set out stools for us all to sit on, and brought out bowls of sunflower seeds and candy.

Once we'd settled in, they showed us around their homes. Their houses were not in such bad condition compared to those I had witnessed in some of the Habitat villages.

They were built in the traditional adobe style: there was a small open courtyard in the middle with wooden, walled rooms all opening up to it. Most had an upstairs, too, where food was stored and extra people could sleep. In-

side, three or four generations of families dwelled in small, dark rooms. Some even had two or three kitchens so that each woman in the household could have her own.

The hospitality in this village was so extensive, and the people so warm and generous, that it was sometimes almost overwhelming. I was invited to everyone's house for a meal, and it was difficult to turn some people down. One evening, five of us went to the home of a woman in her 70's; at that point, we had been invited so many places that we had been politely putting her off, but she had asked and asked, so we finally accepted. When we arrived, we found two kitchens in full use, with four generations of family members scurrying about, ready to cater to our every need.

We then sat down to one of the most delicious meals I had ever had in China: 16-20 dishes of all different kinds covered a table that was surrounded by small stools. The table was so full that we each had to hold our rice bowls in our hands because there wasn't enough room to put them down on the table! And then, as we began to eat, we realized that each dish had been cooked with such care that we could actually feel how much we were being honored; that feeling was in every bite we took. Soon, we were all talking and sharing stories with each other. Two of the students translated for me, so that I could participate as well.

I found the evening very moving. The generosity of these people, people who had so little, materially speaking, was beyond anything I had ever experienced before. Their generosity was manifest in the nurturing food they prepared for us, but even more so, in their generosity of spirit.

That generosity of spirit was present in every moment of the seven days we were there. It was tangible; I could feel it.

When the students had first asked the villagers what they needed, they had no idea. But next morning, when the students saw all the villagers lined up for the toilet, they made a suggestion. It was then that they learned that the government had required them to pave the road from the county all the way up the mountain to the village. All their money had gone into that, which meant that none was left to pay for replacing their aging toilet building (outhouse). The team's inspection of the building confirmed the dire need: there was no roof, and the walls were about to tumble down. Inside, there were six stalls—three for men and three for women. Because this had been the only toilet for 200 people, the line in the morning was long indeed.

So our first student team had helped the villagers build a new toilet building. This one had ten stalls and was constructed of cement block, with a beamed ceiling and a corrugated fiberglass roof. When you stood up, after squatting to use this toilet, you looked through an open window to a fantastic view of the valley and the bamboo forests beyond. It might still have been primitive, but it had its beauty.

Our team then set to work to build a second 10-stall toilet building at the other end of the village.

While the younger men and women labored in the fields, harvesting the tobacco crop for drying, the old men were building the toilet with us. Working right alongside us were both the village leader and the former village leader. We provided the support, shoveling sand and gravel from the hillside using small baskets and buckets (eight truckloads) and mix-

ing together cement and gravel to create the base of the floors. Some of the male students went with the men to the forest to cut the ceiling beams and helped them put the beams in place. Then, at the end, we all whitewashed the walls.

This work was not easy. We were digging sand and slinging cement for hours at a time, and the stuff was heavy. Most of the students had never done this kind of hard work before, so I was a bit concerned. But any apprehension was soon put to rest. Although you could hear an occasional groan when heavy cement buckets were being passed down the

line, no one ever complained. Even more impressive, we seemed to intuitively sense how to work with each other, seamlessly, harmoniously. We spelled each other when we were tired, and often during those breaks, one of the students would sing to the rest of us, or we would play with the children who accompanied us each day.

As for myself, I'd been a bit worried about my own ability to keep up, but I found that I was stronger than most of the girls and some of the boys. What a great feeling to know that!!!! By then, I was 61, but I was in better shape than I'd been in years. The village people themselves were unbelievably strong, even at 70 or 80 years of age. The women, in particular, were so impressive! I watched these 80-year-old women, strong as oxen, carrying heavy loads up and down the mountain, never complaining. Compared to them, I wasn't strong, but I didn't judge myself, for they'd been doing it all their lives. They were role models for me.

As I toiled, I reflected on how empowering this work in China had been for me. It was making me stronger physically, but also emotionally and spiritually. Of course, these are all part of one for me, but it was definitely a physical challenge just to get to the villages. Besides the long, complex journeys involving multiple bus rides, we sometimes still had to hike into the villages or even climb mountains to reach them. But unless we're tested, I thought, we don't know how strong we are. Many of us in the West, in particular, have very comfortable lives. We're not often tested. In fact, we may try to avoid it. But if we aren't tested, we don't discover our true strength, and so may think of ourselves as smaller and weaker than we really are. Again, I felt gratitude that I'd taken the leap and put myself to the test.

One afternoon, two of the villagers offered to take us hiking in the bamboo forest. A group of about five young boys came with us. The forest is watered by a series of fresh springs, which run down through it. These springs are also the water supply for the village; the water is captured into a tank and piped from there into the fields and houses.

The forest was beautiful, with dappled light filtering down. The young

boys put on a show, shinnying up the trees, and further up, we all tried climbing up on the long roots and swinging on the hanging vines. Look out! Here comes Tarzan!! It was a blast. Unfortunately, on the way back down to the village my foot slipped off the side of the path. I landed in a ditch, twisting my knee. Once I made it back to the village, the women came to minister to me, taking turns massaging my knee, applying ointment. Being cared for like this only deepened the connection I felt to them.

Each day, we had lunch cooked for us by the village leader's wife and daughter-in-law at their home, and in the evenings, other villagers fed us. One of those evenings was the night of a funeral feast. The village leader and his wife invited us to attend as honored guests, and we were seated at the center of the long community building already filled with hundreds of villagers. It was an incredible sight: a sea of faces of all ages crowded together, sitting on low stools around small tables. Dishes upon dishes appeared, somehow prepared by the deceased's relatives with help from other villagers. The young men served us all and ate last.

Our last evening in the village called for another banquet, this one in our honor. I sat with many of the women whom I had met throughout the week and two of the student leaders (one translating for me). The women had dressed in their traditional ceremonial clothes, and there was much joking and laughter at our table. We decided that women were the most open and friendly people in the world, and they also decided that I was definitely their sister. I was so moved by their genuineness,

their fun-loving nature and their kindness.
That last night, all of the villagers poured onto the open plaza in the middle of the village. Dressed in their full ceremonial clothes, they performed their traditional dances for us. They sang to us traditional Yi songs of friendship, and we sang back to them the songs we had learned on the bus seemingly so very long ago. As the night and the dancing went on, I felt a kind of energy building, spiraling up and surrounding us all. And then, in the end, there was just holding each other and tears.

Later, many of the students said that they had never experienced so much love before in their lives. And this was true for me as well. Being in this village was like being constantly surrounded by unconditional love. I'd always carried the idea that the world was benevolent and based on love, but this experience of love was beyond anything I had ever known before. Perhaps when people are able to really see each other, to recognize that spirit which is in us all, something very magical can happen, and all of humanity is somehow enriched for it. Is there really anything else to do in life? I have nothing but gratitude in my heart for having had the opportunity to experience this.

As for the villagers, they would light up when we appeared, and say things like, "the village is so much less alive when you all leave." Perhaps the head man's wife said it best when she told me that "no one had ever cared about us before," and that "when the first team left, there was such emptiness." She said she was sure that the emptiness would be greater for her this time, because she had spent more time with us and gotten to know us all more deeply. I realized then that, despite the language barrier, she had become a friend, and that the villagers had to deal with loss when we left.

As for the students, they did not want to leave at all! One shared later that she had always hidden behind a mask, but during her time in the village, she had been able to let that mask down for the first time in her life.

Chapter 11

Unforeseen Gifts

Content with an ordinary life
you can show all people the way
back to their own true nature.

Very often, when we take an action, we never truly know its impact.

We'd come up with a name to describe the student projects in the minority villages. We called it "Villages of Value," to express the idea that there IS value in village life and that much of the developed world, including the cities of China, needed what these minority villages had to offer.

In the spring of 2009, I went with the students to visit two Yi minority villages where we were planning to work during the summer. Accompanying us was a friend from America. The first village we visited was the one where we had built the toilets the previous summer. It was truly like old home week! When we arrived, we were immediately taken to one of the homes to eat lunch. We talked about the summer project and] then looked at the community building where the students would, for the first time, stay for a week in the summer. That night, we all shared dinner. Afterward, many of the women wanted to perform their dances with us again. Then a banjo player showed up, and many of the men also wanted to dance. The children alternated between watching and running in and out. We all did our best to dance until it became too hard. Then we bowed out, and they continued on alone.

As I watched, it seemed that, after a while, the dancing almost put the dancers into a trance, and that it was hard for them to stop once they really got going. But eventually, they exhausted themselves. At that point, my American friend suggested that he and I dance a couple of tangos for them in return. And so, to popular Chinese music played on one of the student's cell phones, we did. Of course, they had never seen anything like this before, and the women, particularly, stared intently as we danced in our sneakers around the floor of the community building.

The villagers put us up for the night in two houses. In one room, there were two small beds. Two of the Chinese girls shared one bed and I slept in the other. Later I learned that one of the beds offered to our party turned out to be pretty makeshift: a board covered with a quilt created a slightly-larger-than-single bed that my friend and a Chinese boy shared. Altogether, there were more than ten people sleeping in the house that night, and it was the only bed left. It wasn't exactly comfortable, but it was what there was.

The next day, after breakfast, we drove to the other village on our itinerary. We had never worked in this village before, but two of the students had gone there previously to check it out, and had recommended that we work there. When we arrived, however, no one greeted us. It was a strange juxtaposition to the way we had been greeted at the previous village. There were a few clusters of young people talking to each other and staring at us, but no one else was around, and no one else came near us. It was a very, very strange feeling.

Finally, one woman came out of her house and invited us in to sit and talk and to have some sunflower seeds, peanuts and tea. As we sat with her, she confessed that she had never seen a foreigner before, and that no one in the village had either. Meanwhile, her little two-year-old hid behind her, afraid of us, until we finally won him over. While we were with her, one of the students went and talked to the young people clustered in the square. He told them who we were and why we had come. They told him that they, too, were afraid of the "foreigners" and didn't know what it would mean to have us there.

As we left the woman's house, the students had finally found the head man. He took us to a kind of community kitchen, while many of the villagers came out to watch and follow us. Before that, we had been talking quietly amongst ourselves about whether this village could really accept us, and we were considering whether to look for another village. But then, suddenly, something shifted. It was as if the entire village, as one, had made a collective decision to accept us. At once, preparations began for a festive, communal meal in our honor, and many of the women rushed back to their homes to dress in their traditional clothes. In the interim, the grandmas showed up with the children for us to play with, and the men sat down around a table with my friend, asking all kinds of questions. The change was truly amazing.

When the meal was ready, about 50 people sat down together, the men at one table and the women at the other two. The men began toasting my friend, and although he doesn't drink, he was obliged to toast back (albeit with sips). They had him try out a large water pipe, too, even though he didn't smoke either. He was a real trooper! The women prepared the liquor for the women to toast, and they sang three rounds of Yi songs, toasting in between. As guests, we only had to sip, though I was delighted to find that it tasted very like sake, much better than the liquor I had tasted at other times.

With this toasting, we knew we were, in a sense, being brought into the tribe, being welcomed as new members of the community. It was an incredibly moving experience, particularly because of how things had begun.

We all then went to the community building where the women danced for us. The village "banjo" player also came out, strumming a wonderful painted instrument, playing more beautifully than I had ever heard before. As the evening progressed, we taught the children to say "hello" and "good-bye" in both Chinese and English in a kind of song, and "talked" with the "banjo" player about his instrument, despite neither of us understanding the other's language. And then, my friend and I again danced tango for them as a gift back for all their kindness to us.

In the days to come, both of these villages would undergo change that was both subtle and profound. They would change in ways we could never have imagined.

When the student teams returned to the first village that summer, this time to build and cover the drinking water pools so that their water would be clean, they found a new attitude amongst the villagers; they were much more eager to improve their village, not just through the help of the students, but through their own efforts. This was something that had not happened very much before. Not only that, but between this summer and the last, improvements had already taken place in the village. Through funding provided by a grant from the government, houses had been plastered and muddy walkways had been cemented. Now the village council was asking if it would be possible to have their drinking water tested, because seven villagers had been taken to the hospital with kidney stones. The students from the Environmental Studies program at one of the universities tested the water and found that the village had been using 10 times the recommended strength of a certain chemical to purify water. The situation was immediately corrected.

The village was taking initiative, becoming more proactive on its own behalf. We were delighted. Then we discovered that the change went even deeper.

The previous summer, three eighth-grade village girls had formed a special friendship with several of the female university students. The students had shared a lot with them about their lives, their studies and their hopes for the future. Unbeknownst to us, these young girls had been so inspired by the students, that they decided to follow in their footsteps. They studied very hard, and when we returned to the village, they had just learned that they had all been accepted at the best high school in the county, one that would prepare them for college! When I heard this, I was ecstatic. It struck me that one thing seems to be a constant throughout the world: all people want to see their families, and particularly their children, live a "good" life, and to take advantage of opportunities that were not available to previous generations.

As we moved about the village, we knew that all doors were completely open to all of us, and there was a tangible pride in the village that had not been there the summer before. We could feel it. This village had been recognized by the students, as a "valuable" place and through this recognition, the villagers themselves had begun to see themselves as valuable.

In the second village, our new village, things began a little differently. The villagers were expecting the students to do everything. The head man had not prepared the villagers well, and the students felt overwhelmed by the task at hand. They could see that there was very little cooperation in this village between families (unlike our other village), and very little sense of community responsibility.

About three days into the project, it began to rain hard, and the students could not work, losing about a day and a half of progress on the new water pool. It soon became clear that they would not be able to finish the project before they had to leave. As the rain tapered off, the students went to the site to assess the situation, deciding they would bring the project as far along as possible, but realizing it could not be finished. Then, as they began working, one by one, the villagers began to arrive to help. Somehow, they had come to understand that this project was not just for the students; it was for them, and the village needed to take responsibility and help.

In fact, so many villagers left the fields to work with us that by the end of the last day, the pool was finished.

It was a moment of truth for this village, I think. The idea of all members of the community contributing to the whole was not a value they had held before. But when the students came to help them, when they witnessed the selfless work being done each day by the students on their behalf, only then did they begin to awaken to it. It was a chain reaction, beautiful to witness: when the students came to understand that each member of society has a responsibility to help the society, then that spirit was communicated wordlessly to the villagers. And then they, too, began to understand.

Like the first village, this village was growing, as were the students.

And it didn't stop there. When the student leaders returned to this village a couple of months later, they found that this village, too, had begun their own projects, working together as they had never done before. When I heard this, I was beyond joyful. At the beginning of our work with this village, I had never imagined that the villagers would be inspired to start doing things on their own. Nor could I have imagined that those village girls, having met the college students, would put themselves on the path of going to college. I was just stunned when I heard. But then, again, perhaps I should not have been surprised at all.

In the end, the secret ingredient—in truth, the only ingredient—was love, and that love started to spiral upward, taking us all with it. That upwardly spiraling energy—always available to us—was tapped into as the students discovered the power of service, as they discovered that it is the way to create a meaningful life. Only when we acknowledge the essential goodness and caring of all people, and model that through our actions, can we grow into the larger versions of ourselves. I think that is the truth of the world, if only we can wake up enough to see it.

After these experiences, something in me changed. When I got back to Kunming, I started doing things likes stopping to say hello to the trash pickers and the man who shined shoes on the sidewalk. These were people we walked by every day, people whom no one noticed because they're considered very low. I started acknowledging their existence, and I continue to do this everywhere now. I acknowledge the people who are selling newspapers, the homeless. People need to know that they are seen. It's the kind of thing anyone can do. It's very easy to be a loving person if you shut off your judging mind. It's a very natural thing, and it's what we're meant to be doing all the time. But I never really knew this, not in this deep way, until I went to the villages.

Chapter 12

Things are Much More than Imagined

The giant pine tree
grows from a tiny sprout.

I had become very close to the student volunteers; I couldn't help but be. Through the discussion groups, I'd been allowed to witness their dreams and visions, and then I'd worked alongside them in the villages and with the projects in the city.

One of the things we offered the students was the opportunity to reflect on their experiences in the villages. Through my service learning work, I'd become aware that all service projects required reflection. That's the only way participants can ever integrate the experience into their lives, by reflecting upon what happened, on what worked and what didn't. Equally important was how you felt about it, and what it produced in you. It's the reflection piece that produces all the learning. So in a typical Service learning cycle, reflection is always the next to the last step, right before celebration.

One way we implemented this practice was to have a sharing time each evening after dinner, whenever we were in a village. Another way was to request that the students write something about their feelings and experiences at the end of every project, whether they had been working out in a minority village or in one of the city projects.

Both kinds of reflection often moved me to tears. Students spoke about how they had experienced a type of love they had never imagined possible, how their sense of themselves had altered because they had gone beyond their limitations, and how their perceptions of people and the world had changed. It is too little to say that the students changed; rather, they transformed themselves. This chapter contains a collection of some of their written reflections. They provide a window into the hearts of the volunteers themselves. (The English has not been corrected.)

I have had a date with EXiDEA through Discussion group since 2007. When I was a freshman, I joined in our DG (Discussion Group) where I met a lot of life-long friends, Susan, Jenny, Lisa and so on. Though we were very new members at that time, they always encouraged us. Hence, from then on, I realized DG is a place in which all participants could express their own thinking freely and learn from each other, and make progress continuously. We get to know the latest current affairs from the hosts each term, we exchange ideas together to deep the issues. We keep learning all these years.

Gradually, I started to attend the volunteer activities held by EXiDEA, from which I obtain the spirit of team-work, and strengthen my willingness to help others. EXiDEA helps me realizing there are still many, many weak people around our community who need our help. We can contribute some energy to help them living a bit better life. What impressed me most is the day we went to celebrate the Children's Day with those kids in Dexin School. They are much politer than those in so-called famous schools. They cherish all the things around them. Even if you just give them a smile and a hug, they think these are the best presents. Whatever things those kids are doing, they are always standing in a queue and in a good order. With the efforts of both their own and the volunteer teachers, they all do very well in their studies. Anyway, just as the motto of us EXiDEA goes "everyone can be a volunteer!" Yes, we can do it. I believe all of us can do it. Consequently, where we are met with the cynicism and those who tell us we cannot, we should respond them with the timeless creed that sums up the spirit of us at EXiDEA, "yes, we can!"

Ginny

The experience of being a volunteer really leaves a deep impression and influence on me. I do love it and it surely will be the memory last forever. I learned a lot, experienced a lot and changed a lot during the volunteering.

So one year later, when I think back to it, vivid memories come flooding back, warmth and good feeling and pure delight of it recurs. I love the beautiful quiet scenery of the Yi people village. It is the blue sky, high mountains, green bamboos, bright stars, silent night, singing birds, running brook, all things that made me relieved and forgot these tiny and meaningless things in noisy city. I can just lie down and enjoy the silence of the nature, the simple and pure beauty of nature.

Wonderful scenery is just a part of the volunteering. There are so many happy moments with my teammates and villagers. I can't forget we named every brick with a funny nickname, which made a sort of boring work so interesting that none of us felt any tired. I can't forget the last night when we had a party with these kind and warm-hearted villagers. We sang, danced and played games together, and actually I have learned some of their traditional dance named YanHe ! These open-hearted enjoyments are so good and unforgettable that I do want to recapture and hold for myself forever.

The most important thing for me during the seven days volunteering is I've changed a lot, including my initial aim towards the volunteering, and my outlook on world. Before the work, I thought I was to help them for they are poor or things like that. However, finally I found myself been helped. People there are so generous, kind and unselfish. Once I gave two candies to a little girl, and of course I thought, like all children in cities, she would be happy and ate them all. But to my surprise, she gave me one back and said we each had one! I was really touched at that moment.

Besides I also remember one night when we had a discussion. Susan asked us a question that is what kind of world do you want to live in. Actually I had never thought of that question before. I always thought world is what it is, we had no choice but to adapt ourselves to it. But that time we all pictured a perfect world in our own mind. We all would like to live in a world of love, kindness, compassion and they do exist and will never die as long as each of make a small change, from saving every drop of water to greeting everyone with a heartfelt smile, we will live in a better place. I believe the more we experience and appreciate the goodness of life, the more there is to be lived.

I rather appreciate this volunteering. Many thanks to EXIDEA, Susan, Jenny and people involved. Thank you for providing the chance. Thank you.

My dream in EXIDEA

Three years ago, on a summer night, a high-school girl who was preparing for her college entrance examination suddenly told her friend that she wanted to engage in charity in the future. Her friend told her it must be an idealistic dream, which was hard to realize. Hardly had she ever imagined her dream would come true in the university.

...t's me, a girl who didn't know in the world there exist some people called "volunteers" until she entered the university. At first, I just wanted to do something like what people in the Red Cross do, I just knew that seemed to be the so-called "charity". But in 2008, when I got to know EXIDEA, my life started to change.

I heard of the name EXIDEA from Discussion Group which is a free platform provided by EXIDEA for English lovers to practice spoken English, to share different ideas and to deepen their thoughts. I was extremely amazed that the members of EXIDEA are almost all university students. They care about the society, they care about people, and they set up the organization to provide a chance for university students who have the same desire and dreams as they do.

The surprise, like a wind, blows away the dust covering on the box of my dreams. I filled the candidate form, in hope of realizing my dream and experiencing something different. I did gain what I had expected, and far more than that actually. I learned to communicate with people actively and openly, not just wait for someone else to talk to me. I learned how to stimulate pleasant and efficient cooperation with team members, and I realized as long as you have dreams you can strive to achieve them. The best present I receive from EXIDEA is the relationship with people in the village. I've never imagined I can establish a kind of family relation with totally strangers in seven days. They are friendly and warm, they are optimistic and diligent, they are open to new things and are eager to learn. Every morning when we walked on the road, every villager, no matter whether we are familiar or not, would greet us with kind smile. Every time when we volunteers had meals together, the grannies in the village would bring their homemade food for us, and the beautiful sisters always helped us with our meals. Busy as they were, they always spent some time with us, chatting, singing, and dancing.

As a girl who is also from a village, I've never had this kind of feeling in my hometown. Though our neighborhoods are all relatives, people can never open their hearts, they often quarrel and fight for money, for interests, which made, more often than not, doubt the so-called good relationship. But in this village, people are just like one family, we cared about each other, and we talk sincerely to each other.

What is the value of village? I'd like to put aside the economic development. I think the real value lies in that people in the village unite together to strive for the development of the whole group, instead of solely considering self-interest. They are interrelated and dependent. It's said the world is a global village. If the world becomes a global village in the real sense, there will be more peace and seldom wars, more harmony and few conflicts, more happy and less sorrow. I think that day will definitely come!

Lisa

The reader might wonder if the students' reflections surprised me. Yes and no. I believe that all humans have a huge capacity for love, but we just don't tap into it on a daily basis. So when you see it actually manifesting in front of you, as it did in these letters, it can come as a surprise.

The students all came from a place where people are generally not seen or acknowledged as individuals, where you're not asked what you think. In essence, individuals are not particularly valued in China. There are so many people, that if a few are lost in a natural disaster, for example, there's not the huge wave of national mourning that you see in some other countries. The underlying attitude is that it's not such a big deal. Families value each other, and parents grieve over lost children, of course, but as a culture, the general feeling is that we have more workers than we need. As an example, I saw highways being swept by hand. The sweepers dashed out into the lanes with huge bamboo brooms, swept a little while there was no traffic, and then rushed back to the curb to get out of way when cars came. And if some didn't make it, well that was just how it was. So, given all that, it definitely surprised me to see how the students responded to their volunteer experience. It told me that we had created something very special, something that went far beyond anything I could ever have anticipated.

Chapter 13

Spirit Of The Mountain

Love the world as yourself,
Then you can care for all things.

In 2008, two friends from Santa Fe came for a visit at the beginning of September, and we took a two-week journey to the northwestern part of the province. Northwest Yunnan was once Tibet and it is filled with traditional villages, monasteries and temples. I had not been this far north in Yunnan before, and it was a wonderful treat for me.

Our trip took us almost to the current border of Tibet, to Zhongdian (now called Shangri-La City), and to the Meili Xue Shan Mountains, a series of 21,000-foot peaks which are part of the Himalayas and highly sacred to the Tibetan people. For the entire trip, we stayed in renovated traditional guesthouses. I'd noticed that something really special happened whenever I stayed in one of those. I began to feel like I was living more like the local people, and in particular, minority people. In Lijiang, they are Naxi; in Dali, they are Bai. And here, In Zhongdian, they are Tibetan. It was, for me, like being in the villages, closer to

something very real, something that had been in existence for hundreds of years. Further, the architectural styles are quite beautiful; all of the buildings have courtyards in the center, and all of the rooms surround the courtyards and open up to them; as living spaces, they feel very peaceful and connected.

The guesthouse where we were staying was owned by my friend's friend, a local Tibetan. It had been open for just two months, following a year of loving restoration and then designing and decorating the place. We were greeted by the flutter of Tibetan prayer flags strung across the courtyard of a beautiful wooden building. We were staying in the old part of Zhongdian, a place of traditional Tibetan houses, stone streets and no cars. It immediately put one back to simpler, quieter times.

Besides the old town itself and the guesthouse, the highlights for me were a small temple and a private house. A very highly evolved Lama had once lived and prayed in the small temple. It is revered by Tibetan Buddhists and is also a pilgrimage place. One monk at a time, from the main Temple in the town, resides there, praying and caring for the place. It was humble, with one prayer room, a few storage rooms, a courtyard, and the monk's quarters, all surrounded by a simple wall. The temple stood on a hill and on the surrounding grounds were hundreds and hundreds of strings of prayer flags and piles of prayer stones.

No one else was there with us, except the single monk, and yet the feeling was of fullness. There was such a presence there, a pervasive sense of peace. On the altar was a very special, forbidden picture, not seen elsewhere in any of the other monasteries we visited. I was touched very, very deeply by this, knowing that Truth cannot be suppressed. This place was truly holy.

The other very special place was the home of our Tibetan guide's friend. This was a magnificent traditional Tibetan home in a village just near the small temple. We were invited in to have traditional yak butter tea, freshly baked bread and yak cheese. This food is a bit challenging to the Western palate, but we ate some anyway. The traditional houses all have intricately carved and painted wooden eaves and the rooms are large, particularly the living/eating room, with carved and painted walls, polished wood floors and a fire pit with stove over it. The friend's mother served us, and we watched while they prepared the space to host a group of foreigners from a nearby resort; these visitors were coming to witness an enactment of a traditional Tibetan wedding. This family also took tourists on horseback rides into the mountains surrounding the village.

From Zhongdian, our trip then took us north. We traveled for about six hours, through some of the most magnificent countryside I have ever seen. The majesty of this earth is

just beyond belief. I took so many pictures, but nothing can really transmit the beauty. For most of the journey, we were surrounded by mountains and deep ravines, navigating over mountain passes at 14,000 feet, and sighting seasonal nomad huts alongside the road and animals of all types wandering freely down the middle. We were told that the snow there in the winter is about nine meters deep and often the passes are closed. I was in awe.

At the end of this journey was Mei li Shan (beautiful mountain). We were told that it was a mysterious and sacred mountain, often not visible because of the clouds. It is on a major pilgrimage route, traveled by thousands of Tibetans every 12 years. When we arrived, we could not see the tops of the peaks (which reach 21,000 feet), but were given glimpses of the glaciers running down the sides as the clouds moved in and out. There is a stupa facing the mountain, and many people were burning incense there and having prayer stones made for their pilgrimage. Prayer flags moved in the wind, as all the while the mountain remained guarded by the clouds.

Our guide, Tsebo, a fantastically knowledgeable (and gorgeous) young Tibetan, shared with us about the meaning of the mountain to the Tibetan people, describing what it was like there during the pilgrimage years. He was a practicing Tibetan Buddhist, so he was able to tell us the meaning of many things in the temples and monasteries, too. He had not been to the mountain himself for many years, so he did not want to take his eyes off it, even sitting out on a deck overlooking the mountain for hours in the cold air as dusk arrived. He had grown up in northern Tibet, in a traditional nomadic family, so we were blessed that he shared his knowledge of that life, too.

In the morning, I arose before dawn. My hotel window overlooked the mountain, and I waited quietly in the dark, hoping to catch my first glimpse of the mountain. And then, suddenly, a golden light lit up the very top of the mountain, now clearly revealed. It was magnificent. Like Tsebo, I could not take my eyes off the mountain. And in that moment, just before the light began to creep slowly down the peak, I was given a profound insight: I knew what it meant for the light of spirit to illuminate a being. I felt completely blessed.

On our return trip down to Zhongdian, one more very special moment occurred. We were heading to a large monastery (one that housed over 500 monks), when Tsebo suggested that we first visit a small nunnery associated with the monastery. We agreed, and proceeded to make our way up a winding, deeply rutted road. When at last we arrived, we found four old wooden buildings, some painted with beautiful patterns and designs. A young nun dressed in deep rust colored robes greeted us, and I could not help but notice that her face was completely illuminated with joy. She did not speak, but motioned us into the main building and up to the prayer hall. I do not think that I had ever seen such a beautiful and feminine room before. The pillars were painted in bright decorative patterns and then hung with brocaded silk hangings. The floor was covered in rugs and deep red prayer cushions. But it was the "sound" emanating from the room that transported me. About 15 nuns were gathered together, each reading different sacred texts at the same time, all in different pitches, and it sounded like a choir of angels. That is the only way I can describe it. We were motioned in and the experience in that room was one of being completely enveloped in love. I did not want to leave—ever.

This excursion was more than just a sightseeing trip; it was a spiritual one for me, a personal pilgrimage. It moved me deeply and changed me profoundly. The moment when the light hit the mountain was like one of those rare instances when the veils are moved aside, and you glimpse things as they really are. I saw that reality is not as it often seems, that it is filled with love, and that love is always available to us. Most of the time, we don't notice the way in which the light of Source illuminates all beings. And many beings are so wounded and therefore so closed that you can barely see their light. But if you look for it, you can actually see it. And then if you relate to them in that way, if you relate from the light that's in you to the light that's in the other person, that's when an amazing connection can occur. Even if all you can do in the moment is smile, something happens, and it matters. I knew that the love I was experiencing in China had already begun to heal me. And now, as I write this, I can say I feel enormous amounts of love around me most of

the time. I came to realize that you don’t have to have a partner to have

that love. That love is there, always, even if you're off in the wilderness alone some place. I don't question that now, and that was a very big thing to learn.

Chapter 14

The Opening of the Lotus Flower

The Master gives himself up
to whatever the moment brings.
. . .He doesn't think of his actions;
they flow from the core of his being.
He holds nothing back from life. . .

In the summer of 2008, through an odd series of circumstances, the head of an orphanage located about four hours northwest of Kunming contacted one of our student leaders. The orphanage director had found herself in a difficult situation, and was looking for help. She needed to raise money for the orphanage, and to accomplish that, she needed to leave for a while and travel to Beijing and other large cities. She had very little staff to carry on the daily workings of the place, so she wondered whether some students might be willing to come for several weeks to help the orphans with their studies.

The orphanage Director was quite well known and respected in

China because of her work, and the student leader felt inspired to help, so he made a proposal to our newly blossoming student volunteer organization. He suggested that a team of seven students be recruited to volunteer at the orphanage, with him leading. The other student leaders readily agreed and the team was quickly formed. In fact, more than 100 students volunteered for this trip, a statistic that floored us all, and made us realize how much the idea of helping children in orphanages had moved the students.

When the team arrived on site, they had to hit the ground running. They were immediately thrown into the thick of things. Essentially, they needed to run the place, something none of them had ever done. In addition, the children were shy and untrusting of these new people in their midst. For the first week, it was difficult in the extreme, but as time went by, things began to improve, little by little. The volunteers were consistently there for the children, working with each one-on-one, helping them with their studies, and perhaps even more importantly, playing with them. And something was happening as a result. The volunteers began to notice a new sense of confidence developing in most of the children. They were becoming more sure of themselves, more open and more loving, and engaging more with the others in their community.

The volunteers often found themselves moved to tears as they watched these children begin to grow into themselves. And then they realized that something very similar was happening with them as well.

When the university student who led the team returned, he was a different person. He had been an engineering student at the Science and

Technology University, but when he came back he decided to do his graduate program in Social Work, so that he could continue to help children who, like those in the orphanage, had lost everything. This alone was a remarkable change, yet not the only one. That year, three of the five students on our central organizing team were graduating, and of those three, two took jobs with NGOs (non-profit organizations). In addition, another of our students, who at the time was a junior, decided that she too, wanted to go into this type of work. She had always planned to work for a large company in Shanghai, but when she was actually offered a job in a management training program there, she declined, deciding instead to continue to work with the student volunteer program.

Another of the students also decided that she wanted to do this type of service work, and later that year, she initiated a student volunteer tutoring program for the children of migrant workers in Kunming. These children were in the lowest socio-economic group in China, and they were the most at risk because they attended the poorest schools and had little support at home to excel in school. Often, they did not have books or even pencils and paper, and they were usually failing in their classes. In general, these children set their sights very low, only hoping to complete the eight years of schooling required by the government before giving up on education and becoming migrant workers like their parents.

But this student leader had a better vision for them. She was majoring in Education at the university that trains teachers, and she knew that many other students in her department also wanted to serve, so she took initiative. She met with the principals of the schools with the highest concentration of migrant worker's children, obtained their blessing, and then set about creating a tutoring program, matching each of the children with a university student. This was one of the best examples of student leadership and empowerment I'd ever seen.

This student leader had first become involved with the idea of volunteering when she went on one of the first village project teams to Ganhaizi. When she returned from her second trip she wrote of her experiences, sharing them with all of us. This is what she wrote:

"As a Han people the trip again makes me feel that no matter which nationality we are belong to, we are a unit, a big family.

Another thing makes the trip special for me is that this is a project developed by EXiDEA alone and I am highly honored that I got the opportunity taking part in the discussion of the project's development. From once a week's discussion of China's villages' situation, what do the villagers need and what can we do for them to the voluntary work we did in this trip I can say we surely did something practical. However what we should acknowledge is that the most requisite thing that a village needs is new perspectives, opportunities, skills and science. Although we can't make a great change of the village's situation merely in a five-day trip, the memory of the trip will be kept in our minds and perhaps one day when we have more possibility to do more things to change we will return back.

Now let my camera move back to the village.

July 26th is the traditional festival of Yi people, the fire torch festival. The hospitable villagers invited us to celebrate in their ceremony party. We were dancing together hand in hand with the melody of Yueqin around the fire. I remembered our team song singing like "We are welcoming a new dawn. The breath changed, however the friendship hasn't changed. I always open the door of my room and I am ready to give you a big hug. We built the tacit agreement. You will love here. No matter it is far or near you are my guests. We are appointed to get together. We leave remembers to you. We have so many topics. We share the air under the sun.

July 27th, we taught the children in the village. I remembered the dialectal nursery rhyme, the songs sang by children, their smiles and their dreams.

July 28th, it was a fine day; we carried the bricks to where the toilet was being built. To compare with the whole building it was a slight labor, but we all had a sense of achievement.

July 29th, the scene of our last night in the village when almost all the villagers get together bowing to say thank you to us, to let off fireworks to see off us will be remembered by me forever.

People in the village are plain and passionate. They are willing to accept a group of university students who are transmitting the sound outside of the village. I've never experienced that I've been appreciated so much and the intimacy been built in such a short time. It's a feeling of being needed, a feeling of important and a feeling of caring. It's a confirmation, a sense of confidence and a departure of loneliness. People are blaming the world is distant. They don't open their full heart to accept an unacquainted person, a new opinion or a new thing, however in the trip villagers allowed us to enter in their place, where they confront their deepest feelings, becomes a storehouse of all their hopes, all their requirements, all their dreams, and even their unspoken fears. When I was staying with the villagers I felt energetic, easy and happy. All they've done make me recognize that what I was doing centered on what is truly significant to me. I definitely want to make something happen, to make some change. And I got excited about archived a goal, I tried my best, I really have done something. And I was disciplined enough to stick to it. This organization urges me to start to explore my own way, a realistic way to dig the trueness, enthusiasm and beautifulness of my life.

The one thing we all need from the villagers and the team members and by far the most important thing in any companionship is trust. I can touch the trust others gave me from the assignment of the task, the cooperation in our work and the communication we did. It's a feeling of safety and I know nothing bad is going to happen when I am with them.

Some people think that it is movies, TV, radio, books, shopping, eating or traveling that drive the loneliness off us. But they are wrong. Only Friends are there to defend us, to support us and to challenge us. I value my friends because they have stuck up for me when others have tried to hurt me, and they have bolstered my self-esteem when I was feeling insecure. I especially love my friends because they hold a mirror up to me and make me look at parts of myself that I sometimes don't want to face. That's what friend does: helps you to change and become a better person. This kind of intimacy is hard to achieve. It takes a lot of willingness from both people, and a lot of trust. How much it was like this between us and the villagers.

The trip told me I was good enough that I deserved a chance, that I should have the courage to sing, to laugh, to dance. The trip told me not to care what other people thought, because the trip was a gift for me, a gift that couldn't be bought. And now I want to give the trip what the trip always gave to me—love, friendship, caring, and most important, trust. But how can I do this in ways that equal it. What I want to give the trip is only a simple phrase. It may not seem like very much, but it is in many ways. What I want to give the trip is a simple, kind Thank you.

If a friend is a gift, the very gift one wanted, her joyfulness is opened in a minute. The gift one gives the other is the gift which one has given oneself. It's the best of presents.

At last I want to use the words of our team song to end my writing: let's cheer for ourselves, because we are great. We all have dreams and courage. We all can create a miracle."

Hu Linyan

(This is unaltered from the original)

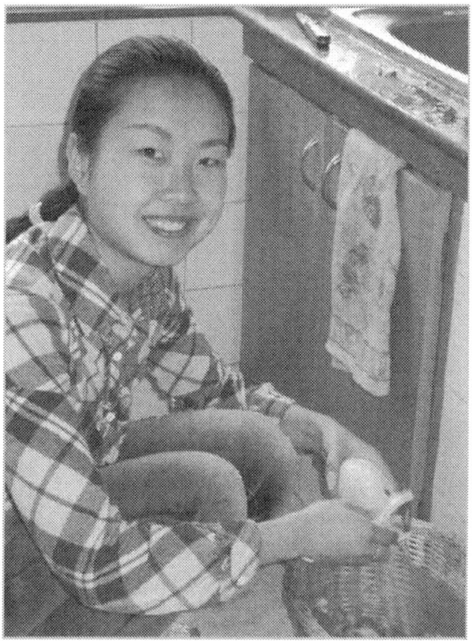

Graeae (Hu Liyan)

By now, it had been more than six years since I first had my visions and began to explore this experiment in China. It has been an incredible journey, with outcomes I could never have foreseen. And then, with the orphanage experience, something more was opening up. The students were taking initiative, acting on their own; I wasn't even in the country during that time.

In addition, the students who went to the orphanage were thrown into something new. They had to learn to surrender to circumstance and then go way beyond anything they'd ever done in their lives. The fact that they had the willingness to do this was beyond comprehension. Through that willingness, they discovered much more about who they really are. And the effect on the children was just fabulous!

It was not only the students who had changed. I continued to be amazed about how my experience in China was totally changing me. I was just not the same person. I had come to find a much deeper version of who I am, a person previously unknown to me and in many ways unrecognizable from the woman who not so long ago had retired and was feeling at loose ends, wondering what to do with the rest of her life. That no longer seems to be a question for me. My heart had been opened wide and filled with enormous amounts of love.

And as a result of that, other things had changed as well. For example, I didn't have to think out, plan and design everything. And I didn't judge people or situations so much anymore. There's a Rumi poem about how life is a guesthouse and everything that comes through the door is the guest. In Sufism, every guest is seen as Source, and therefore the guest is always most important, and that is why guests are so well hosted. Everything that happens to us is an opportunity to say, oh, here's another representative of Source coming through the door!

This is how I choose to live.

Chapter 15

What Makes a Culture?

. . .He (the Master) simply reminds people
of who they have always been.

In 2010, a new village was added to our other three. This one, located only an hour from the Laotian border, was from the Hani minority culture. We were brought to this village through our collaboration with the school for migrant worker's children in Kunming. It was the home village of the principal of the school, Mr. Li, and he was very concerned about it. Because of all the pressures for modernization in China, he was afraid that they would lose their traditional culture, and he asked us if we would be willing to help.

When we started our "Villages of Value" program, we had decided that we only wanted to work in the minority villages because these were cooperative and loving villages, usually poorer than their Han counterparts, and because we knew that the students would have the opportunity to experience other cultural ways, customs and practices previously unknown to them.

As we began to consider this new village project, I remembered my second vision of four years earlier:

I have gone to a village with a team of people to work. As we walk into the village, the head man steps forward to welcome all of us. As our eyes meet, it is very clear that we know each other at some deeper level.

When we have all met and the team starts to work on their various tasks, the head man asks to talk to me in his own home. As we sit on the floor around a table laden with food, he begins to tell me that he has been waiting for me to come, and he is overjoyed that I have finally arrived. He has dreamed of me as I have dreamed of him. There is no difficulty understanding each other's language. This is a minority village, not a Chinese village, and he wants to talk to me about the struggle of the minorities to keep their own cultures and not to be absorbed into the mainstream Han culture.

We talk about finding the essence of their culture, of how to open knowledge of that essence in each member of the village, so that it could always be held in the heart. We talked about the value of the minority cultures and their villages, of their loving connection to the earth and to each other, of their spiritual connections.

My first vision had already shown itself to be manifesting; could the second one be manifesting, too?

Mr. Li had invited us to visit the village, and several students and I decided to go along with him to talk with the people in the community about what was happening. He arranged to take us there in a car, some 11 hours from Kunming, the last three hours on gravel roads. When we arrived in the town, we rested a bit before climbing aboard a jeep that took us up the mountain on what proved to be a boulder-strewn trail. For one hour, we were tossed around inside the vehicle, while we held on for dear life. We went as far as we could by car, and then got out and walked the rest of the way.

The villagers had been waiting for us, and right away several escorted us to one of the houses where we met the head man and some of the other people who helped run the village. Over the next half-hour, many other villagers arrived, including two women in full Hani minority clothes. Several women cooked a large meal, and as it was already quite late in the evening (about 10 pm), we sat down to dinner with, of course, all the requisite drinking of toasts. There was almost an immediate sense of affinity between us all, a closeness that I had not predicted.

The next morning we headed out to see the site of our proposed project. The plan was to create a central gathering place where the village could hold their traditional Hani ceremonies, dances, weddings, etc. During our tour, Mr. Li also told us about the vision he had of creating a small school for the youngest children (K-2). Presently, they had to go away to school with the older children, which required their staying in the town during the week, and only coming home on weekends. When I heard this, I was reminded of the Native American boarding schools. In the U.S., during the late 1800's and early 1900's, all of the Native children were removed from their families and tribal cultures and forced to learn English and dress in European clothing. In a similar way, the Hani children had to leave their village and learn Mandarin. As a consequence, many of them were beginning to forget the Hani language, as well as much of the Hani culture.

Thus, we began to understand the underlying situation in this village. Without a place to hold ceremonies or a school where the youngest children could learn the Hani language and traditions, this minority culture was on the road to extinction. This was to be the fate of all the minority cultures in China, unless the village awakened to the threat and took actions to offset it. But most of these villagers were essentially quite innocent and under-educated, and thus not fully aware of what was happening.

When we finished looking at the designated site, we all headed back to another villager's home for a rice noodle lunch. Then, during the afternoon, we all went to learn how to pick tealeaves which was the village women's main cash crop.

We hiked up the steep terraces to several rows that needed picking and worked for about an hour with the women while the men napped down below.

We had been working quite far up on the hillside, and as we started to make our way back down, I suddenly realized how incredibly steep the trail was and that it dropped off abruptly. I am terrified of cliff edges and balked, asking if there was any other way down. I was told, "No." And then, without any nonsense at all, one of the young men squatted down on the trail, and I was told to get on his back. It all happened so quickly, there was no time to argue. I did what I was told, got on his back and off he trotted, sure footed, down the trail, putting me down when we got to the dirt road. No one seemed to give-another thought to it, and we all continued back to the village. I was surprised that once on his back, I felt no terror at all; only complete trust.

We left the village the next morning after breakfast, walking up the trail to where the jeep had let us off. But when we got there, it wasn't a jeep waiting for us, but four motorcycles manned by four of the villagers. We soon learned that the plan was for each of us to ride on the back of one of the motorcycles for the hour-long trip back down the washed out, rock-strewn "road." In moments, I found myself on the cycle that was driven by my piggyback savior from the day before, and we led off. The road was a series of switchbacks, each about the width of one vehicle, with sheer drops off the sides of about 2000 feet. Again, I had no fear whatsoever. In fact, the trip was exhilarating!

We now understood much more about why this village was in real danger of losing its cultural traditions, and so the student leaders decided that we should create a project to help them. We designed a three-year project, with the first year's task being the creation of the ceremonial area. The second and third years would be devoted to cultural preservation. We would capture their traditional dances, songs, stories, clothing designs and language, and create a structure to support the elders to transmit these things to the next generation. Along with that, we would also create a series of books documenting all of the cultural information, so that nothing would be lost if there was no longer an elder who remembered.

Our cultural preservation trips would take place during the winter school vacation; they would last for two weeks, and students would celebrate the Chinese New Year with the villagers. This meant we would now be operating three village trips a year: one to a Miao village, one to a Yi Village, and the third to this Hani village.

The first team trip to the Hani village was planned for January 2012. I had to go back to the states at the end of 2011, but had made plans to return to China in time to go along because I was so very taken by the minority people and cared so much that these cultures not be lost. But the Universe had another idea. On the 4th of January, while I was in Boston visiting one of my dearest friends who was dying of cancer, I had a mini-stroke. It was the second in six months.

At first, I didn't know what had happened, only that I could not see out of part of my left eye. When I returned to Santa Fe, I saw a doctor who gave me the diagnosis. This was cause for much reflection. When I'd had the first mini-stroke, I'd been in China, and scheduled to fly home soon. It was immediately clear what it was, and the doctors there advised against flying, which meant I was unable to travel back to my family for an extra two months. That first stroke scared me because I had to confront some things I'd never considered before. With only minor exceptions, I'd been very healthy my whole life, and I'd never, ever, conceived of myself as a person who might have a major stroke, let alone someone who might become debilitated, or even paralyzed. So, even though the strokes were minor, they brought those thoughts to the forefront of my consciousness, which was both shocking and challenging.

And now I faced a decision. I was scheduled to return to China, but I knew that, if anything happened, I didn't want to be caught there again, without alternative health care possibilities. I determined that, to my great disappointment, I would have to cancel my return trip in order to attend to my health. That meant that I could not go on our next scheduled trip to the Hani village. This would be the second time that I was unable to go to the villages, the first being when I couldn't go because of the first mini-stroke. It was discouraging, to say the least.

During the course of evaluating my overall health condition, the doctors discovered that I had very high amounts of lead in my body. Possibly this was the result of eating rice in China. Unfortunately, one of the downsides of "progress" there is the high degree of pollution. Businesses, including agriculture, are unregulated, so the food supply is endangered. As treatment, my alternative cardiologist recommended chelation therapy, a method by which the body is purified of heavy metals. The therapy, which took several months, was effective, the amount of plaque in my arteries was substantially reduced, and I was given the go ahead to go back to China. By now, it was May, and I would only be able to stay for three months because my grandchildren were coming for a visit in August.

Throughout the first months of that year, I had been exhausted from the chelation, and I was feeling frustrated and disappointed. I wondered whether I would be able to continue the work in the minority villages that were so dear to me. Because they were so remote, my traveling there was risky. Would my health hold up? Would I still be able to contribute? The loss of Will had been hard, but this was even harder. I found myself going through the lowest period I had experienced since going to China seven years ago. I was filled with doubt and had lost my confidence.

I had released so much of my need to control things, allowing things to unfold, but now the desire to control moved in with a vengeance. I wanted to control my health; I didn't want it to unfold! I wrestled with this a lot, and then I realized that this was just one more test. We may say that we really are going to allow Source to inform us, but when something happens, we get scared. I realized then that this was just another lesson, another opportunity to go deeper in my spiritual practice. Through this experience, I learned to be much more patient with everything and everyone, especially myself. I learned about acceptance of what is and what is to be. I learned not to avoid things, as we always want to do, but to face them, and sort them out. It also taught me a lot about perseverance; I resolved to keep going anyway, despite my doubts and concerns.

After my treatment, I went to China for three months and then returned to Santa Fe for the summer to have a wonderful time with my grandchildren, Everything had gone fine overseas, but then tests found that the level of lead in my blood had gone back up a bit, and so in October I had to do another round of chelation. Once again, I began to wonder if my time in China was over. But by December, I felt that I really wanted to go back for the second team trip the Hani village. I did not know how I would fare, but I wanted to give it a try.

And so, on January 18, 2013, I set out to join up with the team of student volunteers traveling to that little Hani village on the mountain near the Laotian border. This village was the farthest away of any we had ever worked with, and so it was to be a marathon journey. I left my apartment at 7 AM to take a bus to the stop where I was to meet one of my staff people. That would be the first in a series of five buses (and other modes of transportation) that would ultimately, 11 hours later, deliver us to the village where we would be working for the second year to help the villagers protect their minority culture.

As the long-distance bus (our third) sped us out of the city into the countryside surrounding Kunming, I noticed that more and more greenhouses were sprouting up near the city. These produced the fabulous local produce that I appreciated so much. We passed miles and miles of them until we began to get further out into the countryside. The villages and towns seemed to get older and smaller as we went, the landscape punctuated only occasionally by a small city. This bus was taking us to Mojiang, the county seat for the Hani village, still a full three hours from the small town at the base of the mountain. I settled back in my seat, gathering energy for the rest of the journey.

After arriving in Mojiang, we hurried to a small restaurant near the bus station for a quick lunch, before boarding a small, 18-person bus we had rented for the mountainous ride to the local town. It was the kind of bus where you slide off the seat as you go around a curve—and this trip was all curves. Some of the students looked a bit green around the gills, but luckily my stomach held. The views, however, were spectacular. We drank in the sight of the cascading mountains, softened by the smoke of burning fires, with terraced rice and tea fields tumbling down their sides for a thousand feet or more, and village people walking along the side of the road, returning to their homes from the fields. It was beautiful, even if we all had to hang on very tightly.

We made it to the town just as dusk was descending, and there was still quite a way to go yet. Our whole team disembarked from the bus, slung their packs over their shoulders and commenced their two-hour hike, in the dark, up the mountain to the village—with the exception of Song Yuan, the student who was to be my translator, and me. Song Yuan and I were told to stay behind and wait for the motorcycles.

Four members of our team had journeyed to the village several days ahead and had made all the preparations for our arrival. This included making arrangements for two motorcycles to come down from the village and bring us up, along with a couple of the heavier suitcases. As we waited, it got darker and darker. We weren't sure exactly what we had gotten ourselves into, but there was nothing to do but wait by the side of the road. I must say, I was really grateful that Song Yuan was with me, so I wasn't left there all alone, unable to talk to anyone. But it was a challenge for her, too. Because she was from another province, she was having difficulty understanding the local dialect. Still, we could cheer each other as we waited.

At last, two villagers showed up on motorcycles, as promised. They quickly loaded up the baggage, put us each on the back of one of the bikes, and off we went. It was fully dark now, and the dirt road was in really bad shape. It was only one lane wide to begin with, and half of that was so washed out that it was impassable. Visibility was virtually nil; all we could see were the little circles of light made by the headlights as we swerved around boulders and washouts. Maybe this was a blessing. Since I had been on this road before when we first came to investigate the village, I knew about the 2000-foot drop-off with no barrier of any kind. Blessedly, we could not see that on this trip.

About a third of the way up, we passed the rest of our team, walking in the dark, navigating with flashlights, something we would become extremely accustomed to. But as slow as it was to walk, it was a slow ride, too, as the drivers worked to negotiate the difficulties of the road. Finally, a full hour after we had climbed on the cycles, we finally arrived at the village, barely able to stand. Immediately, we were ushered to an outdoor kitchen where we were reunited with our advance team leaders, who

were preparing our dinner in woks over open fires. It took the rest of our team another 90 minutes to get there, but they did, safe and sound. We had finally arrived!

The eating area was actually up above where we were now, so in order to have dinner, our team had to hike back up the mountain. It turned out that we would have to do this for each meal, three times a day, because this particular village was situated like no other I had been to: on a mountainside. This was definitely a challenge for me, but tonight was special: Song Yuan and I were taken up the mountain on motorcycles, and the village head man and the other leaders came to join us—and our drivers— for dinner, and welcomed us with toasts. After dinner, we went to our respective places, Song Yuan and I on the motorcycles that waited for us, the rest walking back down the mountain to the village. There, Song Yuan and I were given a bed to share (a size somewhere between a single and a double) in a spare room, about 8'x10', the other half of which was filled with pig feed. The rest of the team was sleeping on hard, low tables, two to a table, with one quilt each. All the girls were in one 8'x10' room, and the boys in the other. The outhouses were a bit of a way from the sleeping quarters and very primitive.

Everyone was very tired, but the amazing thing is that no one complained about anything, not the walk, nor the conditions in the village, nothing, and it was to remain this way throughout the 10-day trip. I found myself wondering how American students would manage all this. Could they refrain from complaining, let alone remain cheerful?

The next morning, we hiked back up part of the mountain to get our breakfast. When we arrived, what awaited us was a spectacular view, much like what we had seen from that last, small bus, but this time, with morning mists between the mountains and a newly rising sun. We were in awe. This was the view that greeted us at each meal, and our tables were lined up to look out at the landscape while we ate. It was incredibly peaceful, the serene quiet only broken by the intermittent sound of roosters and dogs. Then, of course, there was the occasional sputter of a motorcycle on the way to the town, with Chinese pop music blaring from a portable CD player. Is there any place in the world still immune to this? I suppose not.

The agenda for most of the team that day involved touring the village, meeting some of the villagers and then in the afternoon, climbing higher up the mountain to gather firewood for the cooks. That last task took hours, but they returned with enough for most of the week. The villagers were very welcoming, asking us to eat with them, giving us candies, inviting us into their houses to sit. We were all invited to the head man's house for a welcome dinner outdoors on the cement "patio" that separated the house from the chickens and the pigs and the kitchen gardens. We observed that most of the houses were in good shape, relatively speaking. Only the old section of the village was in need of much repair.

We could tell that the people there lived a pretty difficult life. Many of them were quite old, in their 80's, I thought.

Since the focus of our project was cultural preservation, we set about creating a structure where the elders (or at least, middle-aged people) could teach the small children and young girls about the culture (something the girls were not so interested in learning).

We spent our mornings going from household to household, collecting information about the Hani culture, their dances, songs, clothes, ceremonies and food. We wanted to find out who knew about these things, too, so that we could organize a village team for training the younger ones. We took family photos of each family, and if someone in the family had traditional clothes, we asked them to put them on for the photo. We had been doing this in all of our villages, and it had become very popular. Village families had never had photos of themselves taken, nor did they own cameras, for that matter.

Most had never seen themselves in a picture, and ALL of them wanted their photos taken. Last year, the team had managed to take photos of about half the families, and this year we were delighted and touched to see that all of those families had those photos prominently displayed in their homes.

A few members of the team were designated to gather together all the children and take them to the community house to play and draw as a way of getting to know them. In preparation, the team first decorated the walls of the community house with pictures of last year's trip. Then they went door-to-door, inviting the children. At first not many would come, but we were practicing patience. As the days went by, more children showed up, and then more and more kept arriving. Often, their mothers or grandmothers would come too, many with babies on their backs.

They came to learn and to look at the pictures of themselves and friends. We began to feel a sense of excitement in the air.

We had asked the head man's wife and her best friend, both of whom had traditional clothes and knew the dances, to come to the community center one morning to show the clothes to the young girls. At first, none of the girls were willing to try on the clothes, but then one of our university students REALLY wanted to and did, and after that we could see the girls becoming more interested. Finally, one of the village girls decided that she, too, wanted to put on the clothes. She even had her picture taken in them.

Step by step, things were beginning to change, and in our reflections, we noticed a pattern. Whenever the university students showed an interest in the Hani culture and honored it in some way, the villagers themselves began to do so. We could actually see the shift occurring as they began thinking that the "old things" just might be valuable after all. Rather than feeling ashamed that their ways were "backward," they began to exhibit more pride. One day, as we were leaving, I heard the daughter of one of the teachers ask her mom if she would teach her to do the traditional embroidery. The daughter was about 35 years of age, and it was clear from the conversation that this was the first time she had expressed any interest, and the mother was deeply touched.

In the afternoons, we continued to work on the ceremonial area. We were creating a large cement foundation where the whole village could gather for weddings, dances, ceremonies, and of course, basketball games. (Basketball is an obsession among men and boys in China, even in the remotest villages!) The work consisted of gathering rocks from the mountainside and bringing them to where we were building. To accomplish that, we had to work in stages. First, we assembled everyone, both students and villagers, in a long chain. We had one line of villagers, then a line of volunteers and then a third line of villagers down the road a bit. Then we all passed rocks, relaying them up the line. That task took a couple of days. Then the rocks had to be brought down to the work area in the village's one truck, so they needed to be loaded.

It was hard work, but it was wonderful to be part of it. There was such a team spirit. As we worked, the villagers would sing a song, and then the students would sing one back to them. At one moment when there was a lull, a lovely man's voice floated around the bend from the third team, singing a traditional Hani song to us all. My heart swelled, for I found something very special in this.

The other, major task was to level a large area of ground in preparation for laying the cement. It may sound simple, but it wasn't. We had only pick-axes and hoes, and a kind of leveling blade made by the villagers. It was operated by one person pushing a handle while two people pulling on ropes in the front. We would hoe-up mounds and then the team of three would pull the mounds across the area to fill in the lower parts. Ingenious! It was grueling work, however. We only worked in the afternoons, but the villagers worked from 10 to 5. They only ate two meals a day, one at about 9:30 in the morning, the other at about 5:30. They were amazing workers, both the men and the women, and very, very strong. But our students, untrained as they were and having spent their whole lives studying, worked hard, too, and kept up.

Altogether, more than 60 people participated in these tasks, with each village family required to provide one worker.

There were challenges too. Unbeknownst to us, the village celebrated the New Year quite a bit earlier than the Han, and this holiday was to occur during our time in the village. This meant that we would lose two full workdays, which we had not anticipated. It also meant that the project would not be finished by the time we left. This was something we really tried not to do, because if there was no completion for the team, it was very disappointing for some.

On the positive side, however, we got to celebrate with the villagers, and before that, we were able to watch the preparations. Each family killed a pig on their front doorstep. In the house where we were staying, this occurred at dawn right outside our bedroom door. It was a screaming affair, and quite unnerving for us.

Another delay occurred because one of the elder women, someone we had met on our first day, died the second night we were there. The students were quite upset about this and of course, the whole village had to stop everything to go to the funeral ceremony the next day and then the burial on the mountain. All in all, we lost three working days, and there was nothing that could be done about it.

And for me, there was the physical challenge of hiking up and down the mountain, often on slippery, rocky trails. I fell twice. The students took to holding my hand on the steep places. I felt old and incapable and didn't like the feeling.

Every evening, we held a sharing meeting where each person on the team shared about some special experience that had happened that day, or expressed their feelings about something. Song Yuan had to simultaneously translate for a full hour-and-a-half each night. She was a real trooper and a great team member, and because we were sharing a bed as well, we became close.

Each evening, we gave an award for outstanding effort to one of the team members. One night, they gave it to me for inspiring them while we were working on the leveling of the ceremonial area. They told me that every time they wanted to stop, they would look over and see me continuously hoeing or moving earth, and it would keep them going. They were amazed that I could do the work. I was touched, and that helped to soften the feelings I had been having about the mountain hiking.

We always intended to conclude our work in the village with a celebration. This, too, was something I had learned in my Service Learning work: the importance of celebration. It is an essential last step for any project. So, we alerted the villagers of our intentions in this regard, and as the days progressed, more and more villagers would show up at our kitchen area after dinner. Some came to practice for their performance on the last night, while others just came to talk. As I looked out in the evenings, I could see mixed groups of volunteers and village young people working on a song and dance routine, while another mixed group of boys practiced a Kung Fu routine. As for me, I was working on an English song with a couple of the team leaders.

One night, about eight young villagers and another group of about six older villagers stayed a bit later, and we built a big fire to sit around together. The volunteers and villagers took turns singing to each other while one man played a flute and another, a harmonica. One villager sang us traditional Hani songs. We did Hani dancing around the fire, all of us together at the end. It was quite dark when we finished, but this night we still went on to have our sharing meeting, albeit a bit shortened. It was a magical evening.

Perhaps the saddest thing that happened on the trip was that it poured on the last night, and we were unable to hold the final celebration that everyone had been working so hard on. I feared that there would be a lot of moping around, but that was not the case; everyone took it all in stride. After all, I realized that it is the process that matters, not the end result.

We awoke the next morning, anticipating our walk back up and then down the mountain and out. The trip would take about three hours, and we were concerned about being late for our bus to Mojiang. But at dawn, we saw 16 motorcycles and a four-wheel drive SUV waiting to take all of us out. The group included not only the head man, but also a car driven by the principal from the school in Kunming who had come to help. So, although we'd had no final celebration the night before, the generosity and gratitude of this village was expressed in another way—with motorcycles!

As we began our journey back to Kunming, I reflected on the struggle that minority cultures face in today's world. Each must find the answer to the question: how much should we try to "modernize," and how much of our original culture should we try to maintain in the face of continuous pressure, economic and otherwise?

By now, I had seen three minority villages that were each attempting to maintain their traditional cultures by using it to attract tourism. Each was at least somewhat successful. The first was a Miao minority village in Guizhou Province that had been sponsored by the government to be a "tourist" village. Yet, rather than allowing tourism to decimate the culture as it had in others, such as Lijiang (Yunnan Province), this village had found a way to show the traditional dancing and clothing, and had set up only two small shops for tourists.

A friend and I happened to be visiting this village, a peaceful, normal sort of village, when a small Chinese Tourist bus arrived. About half an hour before the arrival of the bus, a blast of a traditional horn was heard throughout the village. Everyone went immediately home to change into their traditional clothes. Young women dancers dressed in the most ornate and colorful ones, and older women put on more somber ones, all elaborately hand-embroidered.

When we first arrived in the village, my friend, a young Naxi minority woman who had grown up in a village, managed to get us into a house. We were sitting around the kitchen stove with the rest of the family while the teenaged girl was sewing her ceremonial clothes for her own right-of-passage, grandma was embroidering shoes, and mom was taking care of a small child, so we were able to see everyday life quite closely. By the time the bus actually arrived at the village, we were going with the older village women to the ceremonial dance area that the government had supported them in building. It was a beautiful, circular, open wood structure with a large stone pillar in the middle. There were benches all the way around, and an opening for the dancers.

Villagers lined the stairway up to this area, the men holding traditional musical instruments. The tourists were guided up the stairs through the pathway left by the villagers, while the men played the horns. We ended up sitting with the village women, not the tourists, and it was very special to be with them. They wanted pictures taken with us, and then, my Naxi friend tried on some of the younger women's clothes. After everyone was seated, the horns began to play again and the young women entered dancing. They were truly beautiful in their bright blue silk with silver headdresses and bracelets. The dances were dazzling too, and they continued for about an hour as the men, all gathered together in the middle by the stone pillar, played several kinds of traditional musical instruments.

When it was all over, the tourists filed out along the path back to the bus, where villagers had set up tables selling the embroidery of the village and other local handicrafts. Then, the moment the tourists had gone, all the tables disappeared, and the village went back to its normal life!

The second was a Naxi village outside of Lijiang. As I mentioned earlier, Lijiang had been completely destroyed by tourism. All of the village houses had been turned into either guesthouses or tourist shops selling the worst kind of machine-made "schlock" you can imagine, all of it the same. I had visited the old town when I first toured China in 2005. Back then, just a few years ago, it was still a Naxi minority town with many old embroideries and Tibetan things for sale. Many local people still lived there, and it had a World Heritage Site designation. By 2008, however, it was already transformed into "Disneyland," and by 2010, the shops had all been taken over by Han Chinese; the Naxi people had moved to the "new" city. It was a terrible disaster, and I had heard rumors that the UN might take the World Heritage Site designation away. So, to find a village in the area that was trying to maintain their culture—and having some success—was a breath of fresh air.

This village had a tradition of horseback riding and fishing in small wooden narrow boats on a lake nearby, and so this is what they offered the tourists: horseback riding and fishing. The men of the village took turns bringing the tourists up into the mountains on the horses, arriving at a grassy area with a lovely stream where women served tea and small snacks to them before the return trip. At the lake, the men demonstrated how they still did traditional fishing using nets and bamboo fish baskets, and showed how the boats are poled. The very first time I went to this village, I was with Will. It turned out that he had never been on a horse OR in a boat, so he had a very exciting day. At the end, we asked if we could walk around the village and we were taken to visit the oldest member, a 96-year-old woman. She lived in the traditional way with four generations of her family and told us that she still went to work in the field every day. Amazing.

The third was the Tibetan village near Zhongdian that I mentioned in Chapter 10. This village shared its ceremonies, like the marriage ceremony, with tourists, inviting them into their houses for a re-enactment. They too were taking tourists into the mountains on horseback. It was a bit like eco-tourism: providing a cultural experience rather than selling goods.

In all three cases, these activities were bringing income to the villages, while allowing the people to live their traditional lives in their own way. The strategies were each slightly different, but they were all based upon the *valuing* of these villages and of minority cultures, rather than the dissolution of them, and they all appeared to be very successful.

I had been contemplating this situation a great deal, and one question I struggled with was whether it was valuable or damaging to bring new ideas, particularly Western ideas, into another culture. As Americans, or Westerners, we so often think that our ways of doing things are the "right" ways. Yet so often, what we are doing is imposing our cultural attitudes and norms on another culture. Are American values the best values to impart to a country in Asia? Furthermore, what's getting transferred now often seems to be the worst of this culture. Perhaps the transmittal of the values of the founding fathers (which were based on those of the Iroquois Confederacy) would be beneficial, but it seems that we're transmitting things that may not be so beneficial. Is earning more money to buy more things really a good thing for a minority village in China? Many people in America would, in fact, like to return to some of the values held by the minority villagers, such as cooperation rather than competition, or the attitude of generosity rather than greed.

I have also wrestled with the question of cultural preservation, and have come to think that it's not possible or even wise to want a culture to remain as it always was. At the same time, I am convinced that it is not wise to strip cultures of their uniqueness, to homogenize everything and to de-culturalize the world. I'm starting to see the value of bridging cultures in a way that brings innovation, but also allows the people to flourish as themselves. But who am I to say that things should be done in a certain way? I've spent many sleepless nights mulling over these questions and the only answer for me is really another question—what would Love do?

The answer to this question continues to unfold for me, and as it does, I sense a flow of love, empowerment, and mutual exchange that seems to me universal, not dependent on culture, and not damaging in any way.

One thing I do know for certain. Every culture has beautiful gifts to offer us all: each has interesting perspectives on life, expressions of artistry in their handcrafted items and clothing, and uniquely beautiful dances, language and music. When I asked the Chinese students whether they thought the minority cultures brought anything to the mainstream culture, they put it this way: the minorities make life "colorful"! And the world needs color.

Recognizing those villagers, valuing them for who they are and what they have to contribute, has shifted the way I see the world. I have found myself more and more attuned to whatever culture I am in, not presuming that I know at all what is needed or how something should be done, but rather seeking to develop a sense of what might be needed in the moment. If we look at the assets of these people and communities and "recognize" them, if we help the people themselves to value their own culture, then perhaps we will all gain something very valuable, and experience the world as much more vibrant and real. I have been inspired to do this with my photography: to use it to acknowledge the beauty in the people I meet, and share that beauty with others.

I see enormous opportunities for healing some of humanity's really ancient wounds through these kinds of cultural exchanges, and because of my experience in China, this is now so much more of what my life is becoming.

Chapter 16

Connection: The Meeting of Souls

. . .without opening your door,
you can open your heart to the world.

All through my time in China, I was continuously reminded about the connections our work was helping to create: connections between students from different schools, connections between students and villagers, and all of their connections with me, a foreigner.

With regards to myself, the connection I felt with the villagers is difficult to put into words. It continued to surprise me how incredibly welcoming the villagers were toward me, even though they had never met a foreigner before. I recall one time when I went with the representative of another NGO to see one of their Miao villages. At dinner, in a villager's house, the host stood up with his glass and toasted us. It didn't matter where we were from, he said, we were all family. I was moved almost to tears.

The generosity of spirit that I encountered in these villages is something I wish the world would wake up to. We are sleep walking and don't even know it most of the time. Why are we so protective of our "things" in the west, so ungenerous, when villagers who have almost nothing are generous beyond belief? It is a question that I lived with each day and a lesson I took to heart.

The students also found deep connection, with each other, with the villagers, and with me. I have watched students from different schools come together to become one team. By the end of the trips they were deeply connected, so deeply connected that six months later, when they had the opportunity to get together, they were very excited. They would throw their arms about each other and didn't want to leave. One student told me that the friendships she had made with team members were deeper than any other friendships in her life. As to their connection with the villagers, again it is difficult for me to put into words, so I will share a letter I received from Jenny, who put it this way:

"Goodbye Ganhaizi!" with the last loud shout to the village we volunteered in the summer of 2007, which was my first volunteer experience, we left for the city we studied in. However the kind Miao villagers and the children there always came to my mind after the trip. It was the first time that I had the sense of making a difference with the villagers, of caring for people I had never met before, of feeling connected to villagers who showed their smiles and kindness to us. We worked together, building, cooking and playing games during the breaks. It inspired me that I could contribute more to these remote places, to the people who felt being less cared for by the others.

Fortunately, Will and Susan talked to me to see if I wanted to be in or not when they first thought to starting EXiDEA after the trip to Ganhaizi. Even though the society didn't value the university students enough, I strongly believed that we could make a difference to the world with our passion, the creative ideas to solve the problems as long as we could. I still remember how we founded the first EXiDEA project "Light Community," that was all because we cared for the people who were easily ignored by the society and how happy the residents were after we painted the stairs for them. We felt a great gratification from all of the acknowledgement we received and it made us believe that we have not only lighted the community, but also lighted the hearts of the people.

I am always full of great memories every time that I thought about the time working with EXiDEA. How warm the villages are to me from the young children to the elders from the first Yi village we built toilet for. Almost twenty villagers came to attend my wedding which was a great treasure for me. The second Yi village was not suffering from the drought because we built water cisterns beforehand. The scene with the students volunteers not wanting to leave after a week volunteer experience. The great time the volunteers had being together back at school...There are a group of very close friends from the volunteer groups.

I was asked several times why I chose to work for NGOs for the last five years after graduation. Each time I would claim how deeply EXiDEA inspired me, including the central team that worked together, the people we worked for, and the volunteers. I always strongly believe that the process of encouraging more people to care for the world is like the way to make a snowball, it takes time but it is always developing as long as you never stop. I will never know how many EXiDEA former volunteers are taking actions to care for the world because of the experience that they had with EXiDEA, but I am sure that I am one of them.

I talk to my baby who is going to be born in a week while I look through the pictures, the videos, the files from when I worked with EXiDEA before writing this letter to Susan. He must be moved and inspired as well and will become one who cares for the world because of the strong power the work and experience of EXiDEA brings to me.

Jenny, who went on to work for an international NGO, even invited many of the young adult villagers she had met to her wedding. This was

highly unusual, as only family, old friends and colleagues are invited to weddings. This young woman counted the villagers as close friends.

For the villagers, these connections also went very deep, and perhaps this story best exemplifies that. One evening, when the students were making a recruitment presentation to prospective volunteers, a young woman ran over to greet us. I soon discovered that she was one of the students from our first Yi village, one of the eighth grade girls who had been so inspired by the university volunteers. She was eager to tell us that she was now a freshman at a good university in Kunming, as were the other two! Who could have imagined that when we went to that village five years ago to build a toilet, we were also changing lives of villagers in such a dramatic way?

But perhaps the most poignant thing was that she had come to the presentation because she, too, wanted to be a volunteer just like the ones who had made such a difference in her life! I came away from that evening feeling filled with gratitude and awe. We never know whose lives we may be touching, I thought, we can only give from our hearts. Maybe we will not be granted the opportunity to see the results of our efforts, as I was in seeing this young woman again, but I don't think that that matters very much at all. It's the fact that we try to make a difference that matters.

The connection between the students and me had also been profound in many ways. Because of knowing me, they had come to know more and more about the world, and to experience many things that they would never have experienced otherwise. China was also changing very rapidly at this time, and each student felt the pressure of family expectations hitting up against their own personal desires and longings. Sorting through this was quite a challenge for them, and I spent many hours trying to help them find a way to honor both their families and themselves.

And then there was EXiDEA itself. Through EXiDEA, they were connected to new ways of doing things, and they learned skills not taught in school. For example, we did team building training using a primarily experiential approach. Because of the focus in China on rote learning, the vast majority of Chinese students had never experienced anything like this way of teaching, and it opened their eyes to possibilities. Not only were they connecting to approaches used in other parts of the world, but they were also connecting to themselves, to their own thinking, something with which they had had no prior experience at all. In school, they had been taught that there was one right answer, and only one way to look at things. All the while, they were never asked a question, nor pushed to look inside themselves for their own answers. As a consequence, they did not understand that there might be many good answers to a question, or that there was such a thing as "out of the box" thinking which was applauded in other parts of the world. EXiDEA exposed them to all of this. And at the same time, they were learning very practical skills: how to manage teams, to relate to many different kinds of people, to plan and implement projects, and to develop budgets and design fundraising plans.

EXiDEA connected the students to a whole new world of ideas, which was very exciting for them. And it was something beyond that, too: I believe it was a profound meeting of souls.

I would like to say to anyone reading this that you do not have to go all the way to China to create these kinds of connections; you can do so just by noticing those around you and beholding them in love. I believe that we can alter any situation just by meditating and breathing out love into the world every day. If you do this, you can have a positive effect on the world, even if you never leave your meditation room. That's how the world has been maintained for centuries by enlightened beings.

We're in a different time now. Today, it's not about a very few enlightened people working on behalf of the world; it's about more and more people awakening and practicing love. This time is no longer about hierarchy; it's horizontal now, and we need everybody to awaken, to work on themselves, to let go of all their baggage and allow their love to shine out. If we do that, we will definitely win over the dark side, for darkness is just the absence of light. When things seem dark, it's not that there's something wrong, really, you just need to shine a light there. Those who are waking up need to shine their light wherever they can.

Chapter 17

The Joys of Working Together

The best leader
follows the will of the people.

The years rolled by, more quickly than I ever imagined possible.

Throughout all of this time, with the exception of the first two village trips with Habitat for Humanity, we had done everything ourselves. We had every reason to be proud of that, and yet I knew from my experiences in the States that much could be gained by working in partnership with others. Of course, we had worked with the villages and with the community in the city, but we had not fully partnered with another NGO in a collaborative venture. I began to see the creation of strategic partnerships as our next step.

Throughout, my focus had always been on empowering the students, with my serving only as an advisor to them. In that role, I'd point out any gaps I saw in their thinking, things they couldn't see because they didn't have my 25 years of experience, but then I'd back away and let them figure out how to resolve the issue themselves. I took the same approach with regard to the perceived need for partners. I raised the question, pointed out the advantages, and waited to see what the response might be. It was a practice in patience.

Nothing happened for a while, but then, in the middle of 2010,

Chen Xue (Jenny), who had been running the program for two-and-a-half years, decided that she wanted to attend graduate school, and Hu Linyan (who had taken the Western name "Graeae"), took over the reins. Graeae had been involved as a volunteer for several years, so she understood well what we were doing. As she assumed her leadership role, I urged her to consider partnering. Again, nothing happened for a while. It took Graeae about a year to fully get on her feet, but then I began to notice some changes: she began to meet with other NGOs to see if we might be able to partner with them.

Although very much encouraged in the United States, this kind of collaboration did not exist much in China. Perhaps this was because there was always an undercurrent of competition, and it affected all but the closest relationships. There was a deep mistrust of people outside of one's family and very close friends, and although one became friendly with one's colleagues—going out drinking or to KTV (Karaoke) with them, for example—one was never sure that they wouldn't stab you in the back over a promotion opportunity. So, trust was an issue in any proposed collaboration. Yet, despite this, Hu Linyan was open to the idea. And not only that, she was able to find a number of organizations that had goals in common with ours.

The first organization was a large tea company. One of the main industries in Yunnan is the growing and processing of many kinds of tea. This particular company had set up a kind of foundation to support various volunteer efforts. This in itself was extraordinary as there was no culture of corporate giving at all in China. The tea company people were quite excited to meet with us, as they saw an immediate fit. They had already set up teahouses at all the campuses so that students could have a place to meet each other and to study. And, of course, it did not hurt that students were learning about the company's products and also about their philanthropy ideals, but this is not dissimilar to corporate approaches in Western countries. Free advertising and tax breaks have helped NGOs immeasurably over the decades.

At our meeting, it was quickly decided that EXIDEA would hold our English discussion groups in their campus teahouses; it was a simple collaboration, easy to create, and it benefited both of our organizations.

This occurred in 2012, before I left for the U.S. When I returned in January of 2013, I found that another new collaboration had been formed, one with Handa, an NGO dedicated to working in leprosy villages. Handa was looking for volunteers for projects in their villages, and our organization had fully trained and eager volunteers available. Perfect! And so, for the first time, two teams went off to villages in January: one to the Hani village and one to a Miao minority leprosy village. At the leprosy village, the students' job was to teach about sanitation issues, show the villagers how to use new water filters provided by Handa, and help the children with issues of self-esteem. This latter task, in particular, turned out to be a very moving experience for the volunteers.

In most leprosy villages, there are no children, since people with leprosy were forbidden to marry, but in this case, a group of victims of the disease had left the village they had been sent to and set up their own village, marrying each other and producing children. Those children then grew up, married, and also had children. The disease affected none of the grandchildren, but the stigma still remained, and these little ones were bearing the brunt of it. Children from such villages were avoided and looked down upon by others at school. Further, they were often the poorest children and had had no advantages at all, since their parents had never been able to attend school, and they had been so very isolated.

Through this collaboration, the village derived much benefit, and the student volunteers had very deep experiences. All of them became advocates of humane treatment for those in these villages, and for Handa's National Leprosy Awareness Day, they created and performed a very moving play on the subject. Several hundred people came to see the performance, and it raised a substantial

amount of money for the villages. The collaboration was so successful that, in the summer of 2013, a second Handa village was added to our program's plan.

At the same time that this was incubating, Graeae (Hu Linyan) was forming another collaboration. Just before my return to the U.S., Hu Linyan and I had attended a gathering of NGOs concerned about the environment, particularly the use of pesticides on most of the crops in Yunnan province. The attendees included the owners of an organic restaurant and farm, an organic vegetable shop, an organization based in Taiwan that supported sustainable agriculture, a professor at the Agriculture University, and representatives from Handa and Oxfam International. All those attending were committed to creating more awareness about sustainable agriculture, so we began discussing the possibility of forming some sort of network as a strategy for furthering the goal.

Because the idea of an NGO network was such a foreign concept to everyone, no one knew quite how to go about it. Yet, they went ahead, and when I returned in the fall, I was told that they had formed the Community Supported Agriculture Network, or

CSA Network, and that they had started a farmer's market in Kunming to sell some of the organic produce grown in several local villages. Hu Linyan was in charge of the market.

By now it had become very clear that Hu Linyan was a gifted systems thinker who was able to see how different organizations might work together, each in their own ways, to produce a much bigger result. For our organization, she had arranged for student volunteers to man the farmer's market and to publicize it in Kunming. She had also talked to the young men in our first Yi village about the possibility of converting a small number of their fields to organic crops. This was to be done as an experiment, with the goal of selling them at the market in Kunming.

When we went to the village in the spring to discuss the idea, we learned that the Yi villagers were sold on the idea and that they had already formed a group and designated the fields that they would use. By early May, Hu Linyan had found an organic vegetarian restaurant in a city near the village whose owner was interested in the project, and we were able to bring him together with the villagers to discuss the possibility. At the same time, she had also located an organization that gave grants to support such projects.

Things were really progressing. We

needed some additional information in order to fill out an application for funding, so on our second day in the village, we sat down with the five men who would participate in the experiment.

We asked them what their vision was for their village, as we did with every village we worked with, and were deeply affected by their response. They told us that their parents had left them a healthy and pristine village, but that now, because of their use of pesticides—which were pushed on them by the government, promising greater yields—they could see that the land was gradually dying. They were heartbroken at the idea that they would not be leaving their children a healthy village. They also said that they were now working longer hours in order to make more money, and in the process, they had lost the connection with the land and with their minority traditions. And further, they told us that their elders, who had traditionally lived into their 90's and even 100's, were in worse health, and dying at a much younger age. Because of all this, their village was returning to many of its old ways, to organic farming, to less intensive growing for the market, to their cultural traditions and to their original relationship to the land. Then they very flatly said that if they had to choose between money and the health of the land, they would choose the land.

We were stunned. These five men, just 30 years old and with middle school educations only, had seen and committed to a very great vision. They knew what they had to do to realize that vision, too. They had begun to experiment with making good organic fertilizer, and they knew that they needed many areas in the village to do this. But at a deeper level, they knew that things were out of balance, and that that balance would need to be restored for their children to have a healthy future.

And they knew deep within themselves that there was a connection between their relationship with their traditions and their relationship with the land. So, to bring things back into balance, they knew they had to remember their Yi traditions, to relearn the language and reinstitute the ceremonies, and then pass these down to their children. They also knew that they had only a limited time to do this, as the elders were now in their late 70's.

It was inspiring to witness these village people seeing a truth that many in the developed world cannot see at all: that we are all out of balance with the natural world.

To help make this vision a reality, student volunteers came to help the villagers build the needed composting pits, and also clean up the trash the village had accumulated because there had been no way to deal with it. (This, too, is a byproduct of "progress."). The students also worked with them to help restore their culture, setting up an on-going team of villagers to pass on the knowledge, as we had done in the Hani village.

I was struck by the deep sense of trust that obviously existed between our organization and the villagers, shown clearly by their willingness to share their vision with us, and their allowing our teams to help them realize it. This was an experiment, and we do not know what the outcome will be, but if successful, they would become a model for other villages to follow. And all of this came about through the original impetus of the CSA Network's collaboration.

Composting Project

Chapter 18

An Idea Whose Time Has Come

. . .Accomplish the great task,
by a series of small acts.

As we entered our eighth year, I felt very confident in what we had accomplished and where we were going. Our organization, which had begun as just a vision, had now proven itself to be very viable indeed. Year after year, our organization was not only weathering all the personnel changes—new directors, new team leaders and new volunteers—but it was also thriving and evolving. We had been able to grow organically, taking advantage of the opportunities that presented themselves along the way. Our vision of a kind of empowered student volunteerism had not wavered, though projects, villages, students and leaders have come and gone. We had not gotten stuck in fixed agendas and structures, but instead had been able to flow with the needs of the moment. I had never seen any other non-profit organization with quite this kind of flexible structure, and I had begun to feel that we might have created a new kind of NGO, one perhaps more suited to the rapidly changing world we are all now living in.

In 2011, I had begun to see an even bigger vision. It was almost as if something had been incubating here in Kunming, and now it was time for it to blossom through replication in other places.

During my times back in Santa Fe, NM, I had become friends with a group of Chinese students who were attending St. John's College. They were from many different provinces in China. Two of the young men were very interested in volunteer work, particularly in what I was doing in China with the university students. Ji was from Kunming, and Max was from Chengdu, the capital of Sichuan, the province just to the north of Yunnan, and I saw both of these young men in China as well, with Max even coming down from Chengdu during the summer break to participate in one of our village projects. So, when it came time (in 2012) to actually begin to look for another province in China where we might try to replicate the program, I turned to these two, and it was Max who found a potential student leader at a university in Chengdu. After several emails with "Sophie," a sophomore at Chengdu University of Science and Technology, she agreed to put together a team of 8-10 students to form EXIDEA Chengdu.

Some former team leaders had told Hu Linyan that they weren't sure that expansion was the best next step for EXIDEA, but she was willing to try it as an experiment. It says something about who she is as a person that she was willing to do this, as well as how much she had changed since she first became a volunteer. Experimenting, taking the risk to do something that might not work, is anathema in China, for one might fail, and failure is shameful, barely tolerated. Saving face is a huge part of the culture. But, again, Hu Linyan was willing to give something new a try. So we flew to Chengdu to train the newly formed team. We brought with us a replication manual that we had developed. It contained information about all the things we had worked at perfecting over the seven-and-a-half years of the organization's existence, such as how to set up the organization, how to implement projects, raise money, do team building, manage teams, design project plans, train new team leaders, et cetera. We had spent much of the winter designing the manual, and were very much looking forward to sharing it with the new team.

Hu Linyan and I took the new team through two full days of experiential training in hopes of imparting both the spirit of the program and some of the skills. At our last dinner together, the Chengdu team confessed that they had expected the training to be a bit boring, but instead they had found it really exciting! By the end of the weekend, they had formulated an idea for their first project and had completed most of the planning for it. By then, we had all become friends and we set up a monthly Skype call with the team leaders from Kunming. The structure had transferred very easily, and the second EXiDEA in China was born!

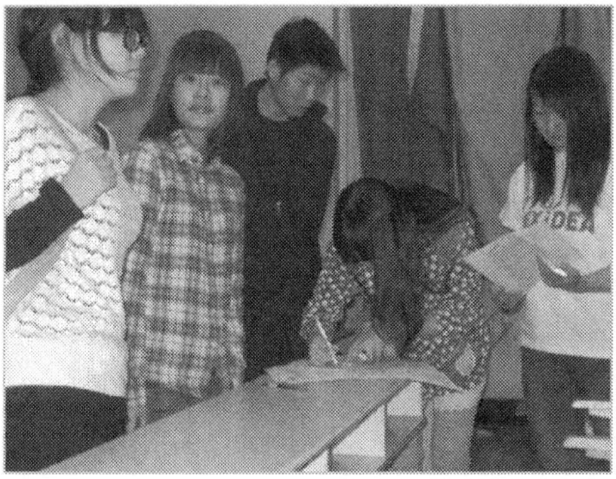

After this, I told Hu Linyan that I would love to see this happen in many provinces, but I could see in her face that this thought had really overwhelmed her. Also, we both knew that it would be difficult and time-consuming for us to travel all over the country to train people. If we did that, we wouldn't be able to do anything else! So we let the idea drop.

Have you ever tried to drop an idea "whose time has come"? It has a way of not allowing itself to BE dropped.

About a month after the trip to Chengdu, during the training of a new group of team leaders in Kunming, one of the girls told us that some friends of hers in Guangzhou, in Guangdong Province, had asked her how they could go about starting an EXiDEA group there. The request just came out of the blue, and neither Hu Linyan nor I were sure how to go about responding to it, since we did not see how we could go there to do training. Hu Linyan sent them the replication manual and asked them to find 8-10 students who wanted to make up the central team, just as we had done in Chengdu, but we still had not solved the problem of the training. Then, as May came along, Hu Linyan received a request from them to participate in one of the summer's village projects. This presented us with a solution. We decided to have them come a few days early so we would train the two student leaders and then have them go back to train the team.

It is interesting to note that these were not the only students from another province to ask about forming an EXiDEA team; eight others from around the country asked, too. It suddenly seemed that the program was spreading spontaneously, without our needing to look for ways to do it. In fact, that year (2013), well over 100 students applied for the summer projects in Yunnan, with only 30 slots available. It seemed that more and more students were waking up to the idea of volunteering and that EXIDEA was becoming more and more known on the eight campuses where we recruited. It was clear that we needed to somehow develop many more village projects in order to give more students the opportunity to participate.

At the same time that this was happening, I was aware that I was being given an even greater vision; it was of all young people in the world participating in what I thought of as *empowered volunteering*, that is, volunteering that the students themselves designed and implemented.

I had also begun to think about how to expand this program beyond the borders of China. I thought that a natural evolution would be to set up programs in the countries near Yunnan Province so that I could use Kunming as a central base. From there, I could support both the China programs as needed, and foster newly emerging programs in such surrounding countries as Thailand, Myanmar, Laos, Cambodia and Vietnam, all of which were within an hour flight from Kunming. The replication manual was in both Chinese and English, so it could be used, at least initially, in countries such as Myanmar and Thailand, where large numbers of people, especially young people, spoke English.

Spirit works in mysterious ways. Contacts began to materialize, and possibilities began to unfold, including the idea of creating a branch of EXiDEA in Bangladesh. At first, this seemed to appear completely out of the blue, but the more I thought about it, the more I saw it as a gift from Spirit, emerging directly out of this bigger vision for young people in the world. Just as the new branches of EXiDEA in China seemed to be materializing without effort, so perhaps would the branches in other countries.

As things progressed in this natural, effortless way, I found myself having to let go of many old patterns. There was the pattern of thinking that I was “doing” something as an independent individual, when the deeper truth was that it was Source that was "doing," not me. Then there was the pattern that said there is an “I” who was not “big” enough or “smart” enough to create something worldwide or to realize that bigger vision. There were also the patterns that told me it had to be hard work to replicate a program, or that I could only work behind the scenes. Inevitably, this question also arose: “Was I able, at 67 years old, to traipse around the world inspiring young people to step forward and take responsibility for the problems in their countries, to open their hearts to the needs of others?”

Perhaps we all have questions like these, and perhaps we allow them to hold us back from being fully of service in the world. I don’t know, but it was true for me. I love George Bernard Shaw’s statement about wanting to be “used up” when he dies. It inspires me to keep going, to NOT let those doubts—and particularly outdated views of aging—stop the work of transformation, both my own and that of others.

Chapter 19

Unexpected Changes

. . . Things arise and she lets them come;
things disappear and she lets them go.

It is amazing how quickly things can change. When I left China in 2013, EXiDEA had been expanding exponentially, but when I returned, at the beginning of 2014, everything had come to a crashing halt. Hu Linyan, who was running the program, was suddenly being pressured by her family to get a "safe" job with a Chinese company. She was also discouraged because funding from Oxfam, much needed to underwrite the expansion, hadn't come through. The consequence of all this was that she decided to leave the organization.

We had weathered a change like this before, and the transitions had all been very smooth: when Will left, Jenny had stepped forward; and when Jenny left for graduate school, Hu Linyan had stepped forward. But now, no one stepped forward.

There were other issues, too. A couple of years prior, the government had mandated that a number of the universities in Kunming move to a "new" Kunming, a state-created city that was being developed some 1½ hours away. As a consequence, our team leaders were no longer in the same place; half were still in Kunming, and the other half in the new city. That meant we had difficulty getting our leadership team together, resulting in less cohesion and fewer meetings.

ely affected the availability of leaders to step forward to

m and the teams.

On top of that, China itself was undergoing huge change. When I first came to Kunming in 2005, it was an amazingly laid-back place. Quality of life was highly valued, ranking much higher than monetary remuneration, and the people were extremely friendly, stopping you on the street to try out their English, or including you in their dancing. But now, no one made eye contact when they walked down the street, and the competition for high-paying jobs was intense. The students had changed, too.

When I'd first came to China, most of the students I met were the first in their families to go to university, and so they were also very innocent in their outlook. A program like ours was very, very new to them, and they were excited to learn everything about it. But by 2014—in such a short period of time—students seemed very different. Whereas the students I first met were incredibly grateful to their families for the substantial sacrifices they'd made in order for them to get an education, students now were beginning to feel entitled. This next group had had more money growing up. They had been indulged, so they were also more jaded, more worldly, and less excited by new ideas. In addition, the universities were now beginning to offer student volunteer opportunities, though the programming was quite superficial (usually only one day long), and it was not *empowered* like ours had been. It did not involve students in the planning and implementation. But again, competition held sway. Volunteering was no longer as meaningful and potentially life altering; it had been reduced to something to put on your resume.

Obviously, these changes had all been building little by little, but by 2014 they all came together in one fell swoop, and shifted the entire context. I found myself having to do much soul searching, trying to decide what to do. I loved what the students and I had created together, and loved the students and villagers I had met over the years. I had loved this all so much that I had invested significant amounts of my own money into it, but that was no longer an option. Of course, I wanted EXIDEA to continue on and to grow, but it was clear that it couldn't go on without external financial support, and certainly not without student leaders.

I knew I had to let go.

That decision, once made, left me with many doubts. I started second-guessing myself, questioning our success, looking for where we had gone wrong, and playing out "what if" scenarios. Yet, one morning in my meditation, a different view was presented.

Clearly, the program had transformed hundreds of students over the years; of that, there could be no doubt. It had opened their hearts, expanded their thinking, empowered them and changed their view of life. Students who had never even heard of the concept of volunteering before now knew that service was key to a meaningful life—and a meaningful life was terribly important to them. They had also learned to think for themselves, and to collaborate. Not only that, they had gained many new and useful skills in the arena of project management and community organization. The people in the villages had transformed too. The caring exhibited by the student volunteers had touched them deeply and ignited their own empowerment. Because of our efforts, they had come to value themselves more; they took pride in their cultural traditions, took more initiative and responsibility, and the circumstances of their lives had improved.

And now, as I sit here in the U.S. writing this book, I have a deep trust that those eight years in China were valuable for all who participated, that we made a difference. To distill it down to its essence, we all had the opportunity to love each other and to bring more love to the planet, and we did so for close to eight years. Isn't this what life is really all about; bringing more love to the planet? When I looked at it this way, I began to see just how amazing the whole program had been.

We never know what impact we may have had on the world. Did those hundreds and hundreds of students and villagers who participated in the program then go on to have a positive impact on others? What happened in other provinces when the students went back to their homes or on to graduate school or a job? We just don't know.

My work in China had run its course; that cycle was over, and a new one was just beginning. My experience in China enabled me to come away with a working model for my empowered volunteering approach: community-based service programs that are designed and managed by students. I am now beginning a new program, which I am envisioning as worldwide, using the model developed over the years in China as the basis of it. The lesson here is that nothing is ever wasted; we must just learn to let go when the cycle is over, and let the future unfold into the present moment.

When I mentioned to Jenny that I had almost finished writing this book, she told me that one of the original volunteers was also writing a book about his experiences with the projects. She asked if she could get my book translated into Chinese and publish it there in tandem with the volunteer's book, suggesting that this could start a whole new wave of interest in deep volunteerism and student leadership. We just don't know what will happen in the future.

Chapter 20

The Return

The Master can keep giving
Because there is no end to her wealth.

I knew it was time to leave China and to return to my home in the U.S., to reflect upon all that I had learned, to integrate all my experiences and consider how I might be of service in the future.

I made my preparations, and began saying good-bye to everyone who had meant so much to me there.

Then, one evening, after a delicious dinner of Yunnan hot pot with my friend Su Yao (Susan) and some last minute shopping together on the crowded street of little shops nearby, I decided to take a last stroll through Green Lake Park. It was a beautiful, warm night, and even at 9 PM the park was full; hundreds of people were strolling arm and arm, as if choreographed for my benefit. As I made my way, I came upon a very exuberant group of about 10 people dancing around in a circle, singing joyously and playing traditional Chinese three-stringed instruments. A crowd had formed under the trees to watch, caught up in the enthusiasm, tapping their feet and moving with the music. I remember the scene like a beautiful snapshot, the light from a single streetlamp filtering down through the leaves, falling on both the dancers and the audience, everything else hidden in shadows.

That evening felt like many evenings I'd experienced when I first arrived, before all the changes. It reminded me of when I first noticed how the people here seemed to derive so much joy from such simple pleasures. Perhaps, just for tonight, everything had returned to that simpler time.

Then, as I walked on, I found a group of about 60 women dancing with their silk parasols. Again, the dancers were illuminated by a single light, and it was as if the scene had been orchestrated by a master filmmaker. I moved closer to get a better view and there, in the front row, was a little girl of about eight, dancing with all the women. She knew every step, every move of the parasol. I stood transfixed, watching this mesmerizing little girl, so confident in herself, so free to participate with all the others, out at 9 PM in the middle of the week . . . dancing her little heart out.

A little girl dancing her heart out . . . This is what it looks like, when we live as we are meant to live, I thought: when we are living life to its fullest, expressing who we truly are, letting others see our beauty, our grace, our love. May we all come to know what it is to dance our hearts out, just like this little girl.

I returned from China with a heart full of many gifts, not the least of which was this image, and this wish. I have spent much time contemplating how my experience in China transformed me. I certainly learned a great deal about other cultures. Through spending time and interacting with both the mainstream Chinese and minority people, I am no longer only an American, but more a world citizen, something that both Jenny and Will also noticed about themselves.

It is also clear that my years in China opened my heart, enabling me to love more fully and without judgment. I have learned to have extraordinary patience (something that I have struggled with for much of my life), and I have learned how to stay in my heart no matter what is happening, even when it doesn't look like things are working out, or when I am shocked by change. And I have learned how to be reverently grateful for all that is given.

Many things were deeply challenging, and these experiences also instructed me. There is nothing quite like the loneliness one experiences when, as a foreigner, without language, one finds oneself sitting at a large dinner table where many people are engaged in lively conversation for hours, everyone having forgotten that you need a translator in order to participate. Many times, I felt helpless or dependent, and always, there was the endless waiting: waiting for buses, people, meals, and of course, translation. And then there were the losses, not just of Will, but of Jenny too, when she left Kunming for Beijing to take a new job with another NGO and to go to graduate school. Then there was the loss of Hu Linyan, and finally, the loss of EXiDEA itself. These losses each ripped open my heart, again and again.

All of these things were very, very challenging, yet they taught me so very much. I returned with a newfound appreciation for community and connection in all its aspects: how much we all need it, how much we all long for it. The experience in China also confirmed my commitment to service. I know now, with certainty, how much it nurtures everyone:

both those who serve and those who are served.

Prior to this, I had been very committed to community service, especially Service Learning for young people. I had held administrative positions in this field for some time, and I had initiated many Service Learning projects, but had never had the opportunity to experience the whole process myself. In China, I did. Together with the students, we took each project through the whole cycle, from visioning to manifestation to reflection and then celebration. Through this, I developed a deep appreciation for all aspects of the project cycle. Not only that, but I also saw the program undergo the more challenging aspects of its evolution. We found collaborators and built effective partnerships in preparation for expansion and replication before recognizing that circumstances were calling for a different response. Then, rather than trying to hold on in the face of too many obstacles, we made the conscious decision to create closure, releasing EXiDEA so that it might be reborn in a new form, and a new cycle might begin.

Thanks to this experience, I have developed a new, more robust model for how to do international projects of this nature. It is a holistic, vision-based process of project development, and it rests on empowerment and collaboration. The work in China reinforced the idea that those who would lead projects of this type need a full spectrum of skills, ranging from the capacity to engage with others to create a shared vision, to the practical skills involved in bringing that vision into manifestation.

I have also become convinced that work of this nature requires a strong spiritual foundation, though this is often missing from our thinking. By "spiritual foundation" I do not mean dogma or missionary righteousness, but quite the contrary. I mean rather a willingness to seek out what is right for all concerned, to be open to what "is wanting to occur", rather than imposing our will or our singular vision. It is a willingness to go beyond our minds and our egos, a capacity to listen to the hearts of others, as well as our own. Another way of putting it is to say that the work must be Source-based; it must emerge out of and be guided by a sensibility that transcends individual ego. It is important to continuously attend to the flow of energy, to refrain from imposing one's will, and to wait to be shown how things want to unfold. This is a universal wisdom principle. In China, this was once known as the practice of listening to the Tao. Because of the political climate there, it was not possible to have a spiritual dialogue *per se* with the students at this time, but their words conveyed the feeling nonetheless: "I felt it in my innermost heart," they would say. Yes.

I returned from China with the ability to throw myself passionately into the moment, letting go of any expectations regarding the outcome, and allowing things to flow in a more natural way, trusting that if I am awake to the moment, I will know the next step to take. I call this "passionate non-attachment." Perhaps this came about simply because I had been in a foreign country without knowing the language. I had to trust much more than I did when I was at home, in a familiar place with familiar people.

I returned also aware that my third vision—which featured young children about the age of that little dancer—had yet to materialize. As of this moment, I still wonder what that vision meant, and where it might lead me.

Epilogue

The World IS Changing

The more powerful it (a country) grows,
the greater the need for humility.

One of the benefits of living a long time is that you can see more readily the consequences of actions, and how things are shifting and changing.

I grew up in a time when the U.S. "military/industrial complex" was just beginning to become powerful. I actually remember President Eisenhower warning us about the potential problems this could cause America.

Then, in the late sixties, I marched in the anti-Vietnam war rallies and worked to end this conflict and bring our soldiers back home. I saw how many people were lost during that time, both soldiers and Vietnamese civilians, and how damaged the ones who survived were when they made it back. And in the years since, I have observed the U.S. misusing its great power—bullying others in the world, damaging the Earth, and succumbing to the fear of terrorism—and this has spurred me to work toward change. Many throughout the world are suffering, whether as a consequence of our actions over these past 60 years, or because of huge natural disasters like the earthquakes in China, Pakistan, Chili and Haiti, or as a result of climate change, as with the devastating typhoons in Indonesia or, closer to home, Hurricanes Katrina and Sandy. Many people live in abject poverty, children starve or die of disease before their 5th birthday, and many elders are left to live the remainder of their lives in extreme loneliness.

Is this the world we envision for our children? I think not.

At the same time, I have felt a stirring, perhaps the early indicator of a deep shift occurring throughout the world, and particularly in the United States. It seems that our nation is in need of more humility, just as the Tao says, and in recent times, we have witnessed what many take to be the erosion—or even collapse—of several of our structures and systems, our educational and healthcare systems being prime examples. Though challenging in many ways, these changes may be indicators of a deep change in our consciousness. As a case in point, our economic crisis has had some positive effects: people are downsizing, buying and consuming less, and re-finding what truly matters to them. They are enjoying simple pleasures, more time with their children, music and dance.

Likewise, over the years, I have been deeply moved by the incredible outpouring of generosity that occurs whenever there is a natural disaster. Many even rush to the site to help in any way they can, and many more gather food, clothes and funds to help those who have been left with nothing. Yet, I have also watched these efforts peter out as the worst of the disaster lessens, and the victims return to their everyday forms of poverty. There are thousands of NGOs in the world, all doing wonderful work, none of it ever enough.

Witnessing all this, I have often contemplated what could possibly turn this around. What would truly work to create the world we all dream of?

In 1994, I started a non-profit organization called the Center for Service Learning Opportunities in Education, an organization dedicated to creating training programs to encourage and support students to learn through service to their communities. I was very committed to the concept of Service Learning, though I had not yet fully realized what its potential was.

Then, one day, I was participating in a river restoration project that I had helped organize. The project involved about 50 children, 5th and 6th graders from a local elementary school. Their job that day was to begin to restore a riparian habitat on a site along the river. The land had been overgrazed, and so had become completely bare of vegetation. It was desolate and barren without any sustenance for nesting birds or other wildlife. The students' task was to cut and plant willow stands along the riverbank. The area of damage was at least a mile long, and we only had about two hours to work on it. I didn't think we could make much of a dent in that time, so I was already thinking ahead as to how many more groups of students would need to be brought to the site to help. But then, as the day progressed, something surprising happened. I stood back and watched in awe as the entire riverbank seemed to come to life, re-planted, with much joy, by the students. Not only that, but there was still time, at the end of the day, for the students to share their experiences with each other!

I think that it was on THAT day that I saw for the first time, the power of young people, working together, to change the world.

What would happen, do you think, if all the young people of the world began to work on the problems in their own countries? What if millions of university students worked in teams to help their villages, their communities, the environment or the children who live in their piece of the planet? What would the world be like?

In many Third World countries, and even in countries like China—which is part First World and part Third World—the university students of today are, aside from a few of the privileged, the first generation to become well-educated people. These university-educated students are bright, hardworking, creative, enthusiastic, idealistic, and full of energy. With some guidance, they can also be helped to open their hearts, to care about what is happening to others less fortunate in their own countries. This has happened in China, and it can happen in every country of the world. The old world is dying; the new must be created through new thinking and a new kind of caring. We must grow out of a world preoccupied with conspicuous consumption, greed and violence, to one characterized by conspicuous caring.

It has been many years since my first awakening to the power of the young. Since that time, thousands and thousands of children throughout the US and other Western countries have benefited from such programs, and through them, they have become part of the solution for their community's problems. And the idea itself has continued to grow. The NGO I founded is now named **The Center for Intercultural Education,** and our work is in the Third World.

One day, I realized the power of young people to change the world. But what of older people? What can we do? These two moments in the life cycle, youth and elderhood, have some important similarities—and these can be the basis for a natural, and very mutually beneficial, alliance. I believe that we, as Elders, have a natural role to play, as mentors and guides to those who are younger and lack our hard-earned experience. And when these two generations come together in the spirit of service, that special alchemy can bring more light and love into the world. As a way of demonstrating that, I would like to include a letter I received from Will as I was working on this book:

When I was trying to start writing about how Susan affects me as a young Chinese in last 9 years, I suddenly realized that I couldn't even make a start of it. After having her invitation, I can't remember for how many times that I opened my computer and then closed it for nothing written. I really don't know how my 9-year growth linking with her can be concentrated into just these pages. So I started to recall nearly very moment that I've been with her and tried to dig out those most important parts for me. And Maybe I can start with this one:

Follow the Heart

It sounds like a cliché for many people but really meant a lot to me 9 years ago and even up today. I met Susan at an English Corner in Kunming in about early 2006. In following couple of weeks, we had a lot of wonderful conversations. We talked about University students, NGO and minority culture. I could tell that both of us were excited and believing about what we've talked. Because of these conversations, in the following 3 years, we've worked together for many meaningful programs including creating and developing EXIDEA. These 3 years was the happiest life episode I've ever had. However, after graduation, I confronted a dilemma between my personal passion and family responsibility. On one hand I enjoyed and were passionate about what Susan and I were doing, on the other hand, my mom alone was running a small shop to financially support the whole family for more than 20 years, which was very hard for her. She ran the shop 365 days a year and even dare not to have a break when she got sick. Susan noticed my difficulty and shared her viewpoint with me that for the big life turning point, I should listen and follow my heart. Thanks to her support, I decided to take a job offer working aboard for a China state-owned construction company and started my oversea career in 2008. Although I couldn't work together with her, my oversea job substantially released our family financial pressure in last 7 years. My mom now unfortunately got pancreatitis. Sometimes, she closed the shop without big pressure when she's feeling not well. To be frank, Susan paid a lot of time, energy and money on helping me to become a qualified organizer and team leader. I believe if she only gave me a slight pressure, I couldn't refuse her, which would definitely have changed my life path in general. However, she didn't do like that but encouraged and supported me to follow my heart. Looking back what I've done for my family, I am proud of my choice at that time and deeply appreciate Susan's enlightenment and encouragement for me.

Pragmatically speaking, 9 years ago even for me, I couldn't understand Susan's motivation of staying in China very well. A single American women paying everything for years to support students there and expecting nothing practical from them, it really makes herself suspicious. I even once wildly thought that she might be a secret agent carrying important political mission from America, like it was always appeared in movies. However this wild guess has never come to reality.

She is always a common foreigner and we are just normal Chinese. Before, I often asked Susan: "would you miss your family and how could you bear to leave them for such a long time." She told me:" Yes I do miss them and they are important to me. But I feel that my heart is here and what I am doing here is more important" I was really moved by her words. Choice of our heart sometimes may not be easily understood by people around us. But it doesn't matter, you work for what most important to you. She not only supported people including me to understand and follow our inner heart but also use her own choice to best interpret this valuable life principle to us.

Trust

The moment she told me: "I would like to put you in charge of all volunteer programs in Yunnan", imagine as a student, how trusted I could feel. It happened nearly 9 years ago, but is still very vivid to me today. Susan meant what she said. She did let me lead the team. More importantly, even if sometimes my thought was not matured enough, she tried to help me translate a potential into a capacity instead of directly intervening. Later on, we made a big success and have more and more excellent students to join us together with their heart. EXIDEA grow. Many years later, when I, as a manager, have the chance to lead a team again in my company, I naturally trust every team member whom I chose. I can see how important and effective this true trust can bridge the communication among us. Because of such trust, my colleague and I together again and again broke through many difficult job tasks and have been recognized by the industry.

Brave

I started to join my company as a site translator at age of 22 and then speedily grow up as a site office administrator, assistant project manager, project manager and now deputy general manager for the company in East Africa region at age of 29. I hadn't been grant much time to stay on one position. It normally only allowed me about two years for each promotion. To be frank, besides excitement I felt more uncertain about myself. Facing an unfamiliar position and a group of staff members who are mostly elder and more experienced than I am in the field, it's not just a challenge but real pressure. Then I thought of Susan. She always believes that young people could solve the problem and do much better than they thought. That's why we started EXIDEA, to give students a live platform to realize their ideas. We began with nothing but faith and end it up with a real-hearted impact on students of thousands. It's an accomplishment. The situation that time in Kunming was much more difficult than now. After thinking of this, I felt to have much strength to being forward.

Following the heart, truly trust your team members and being brave & persistent to your undertaking are no special and secret to any of us. But I spent almost a decade to deeper understand how important it is for a person's life as well as his heart. As one of the youngest company regional GM, now I am managing seven projects across Kenya, Uganda and South Sudan, with total contract value of more than USD 300 million. It's hard to say if it is a big success for a person's growth but it's for sure a perfect reflection of Susan's belief that young people can solve the problem and do much more and better than they thought.

My understanding and ownership of Heart, Trust, and Brave are the best gifts that Susan has been giving me.

I think that there must be at least one person in most people's heart. You think of him or her when you confront uncertain future, difficult time, or even dark moment in your life. You would imagine what he or she would think or do if they were in the same situation as you. Thinking of her, then you are lighted and suddenly know how to do next. Susan is such person to me.

I am quite blessed to meet her in my early age, as a value teacher and mostly, a very special friend of mine.

Gifts from My Journey of Service

As I said, my journey gave me many gifts. Here I would like to share some of the things I learned along my path:

- People everywhere, regardless of culture, hunger for soul connections, for experiences and relationships that honor them and help them discover who they truly are. In China, this was as true for the students as it was for the minority villagers. I believe it is a universal longing.

- Visioning is important at every level: at the world level, the national level, the community level, the project or organization level, and the personal level. Visioning should be an important part of any project, and developing a *shared* vision is essential for real success.

- Our visions should not be limited by what we think we can achieve. We tend to put limitations on our visions, and on ourselves. When I was given these visions, I could have said I'm too weak, but I wasn't—and neither are you. We just *think* we're small. Your visions will not ask more of you than you are capable of.

- People's individual visions naturally follow the gifts they were born with. We're given all the things we need to accomplish whatever we are called to do; we just have to look at what we know. Everyone comes in with a gift and a purpose, and we naturally grow in that direction. Perhaps, because I was older, I doubted my capacity at first. But I was shown a vision, and by trusting in that vision, a path opened for me.

- We're often blind to the larger patterns at work in our lives and in the world, so we don't see how everything that has happened in our life was necessary to bring us to where we are right now. This is the practice of gratitude; try to be grateful for everything, even the seemingly painful things.

- Go in the direction of your pain. People tend to run away from their trauma. My spiritual teacher says that pain is a calling card to life. If you are wounded in some way, consider service. Service can heal you.

- Service is a way of giving back in recognition that we, ourselves, are always being served, if we're awake enough to notice. It is our job to wake up to that truth.

- Everything is valuable to the inner journey; loss strengthens us if we allow it to. China taught me that life is an adventure with no end destination. As the Tao so clearly teaches us, it is by walking the path with grace and patience that we come to know more fully who we really are.

- It's not advisable to plan everything out before beginning. I've learned that we're not shown more than the next few steps ahead; that is how visions work. This matches well with what is happening in the "real" world today: Things are changing too rapidly now for us to have five-year plans. We have to read the energy of whatever is happening in the moment, and learn to flow with it. In a sense, we must all learn to live in the Tao.

Once, many years ago, I made a pilgrimage to the great cathedral in Chartres, France. I was eager to walk the ancient labyrinth that had been set into the floor, but when I arrived, I saw that it was almost entirely covered with folding chairs, a reminder that the cathedral is also a fully functioning Catholic Church. I decided to come back in the morning, hoping that the chairs would not be there. Unfortunately, the chairs were still there, but I decided not to let them stop me. I began walking the labyrinth, moving aside each chair as I went, and then placing it back in its position. Working like this, I could only see a few steps ahead at any one time, and so it was a complete surprise when I reached the center. And then I was rewarded by a glorious stream of light coming in through one of the many magnificent stained glass windows. As I stood there, bathing in that healing light, I noticed that the space all around me had become very hushed and quiet, as if all the other visitors had decided to respect my process. In that moment, I was reminded of the importance of process. As Westerners, we tend to focus our attention on the outcome or the goal, but it is more often the process itself that matters. *We cannot see more than a few steps ahead. Take those steps and trust that the next steps will be shown, in the right timing. Do not force or impose your will.*

Villagers

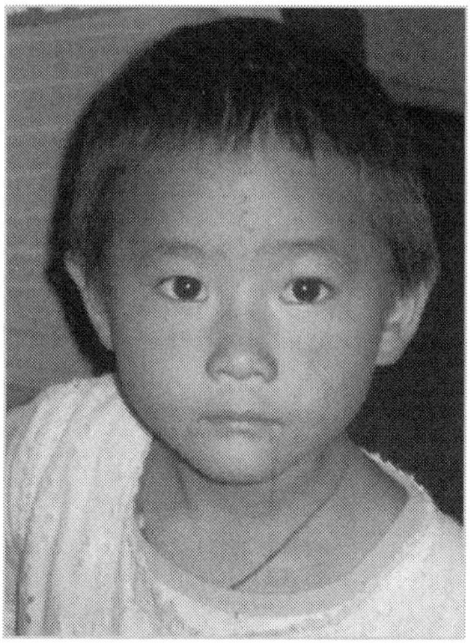

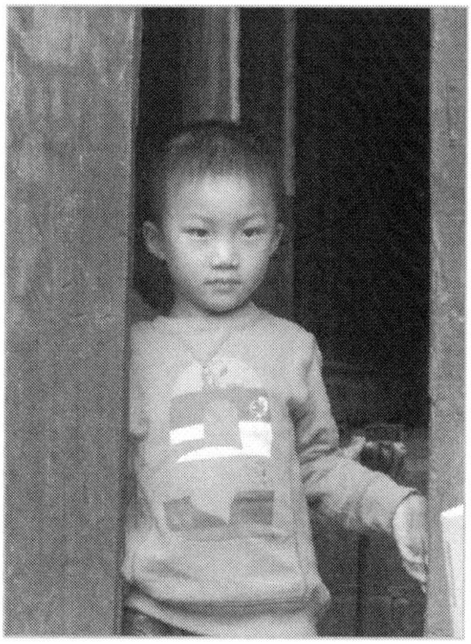

Acknowledgments

I wish to especially thank Will (Zhan Can Wei), Jenny (Chen Xue), and Graeae (Hu Linyan), the Chinese students, who, over my 8 years in China co-created and ran the program. Without their generosity and enthusiasm, nothing would have happened.

I also wish to thank my incredible editor, JoAnne O'Brien-Levin who held my hand throughout the process and kept me going when I wanted to give up; Jonathan Smith who kept saying "You ought to write a book about all of this"; Lyn, Jim and Prisma Avery, who went with me to China so that I could find out if the visions were true; my incredible family who let me miss holidays, birthdays, and daily contact; Habitat China, without whose sponsorship and support I could never have made it into China, and all the Chinese student volunteers who took the chance to give from their hearts to total strangers. Lastly, I want to thank my late partner, Bruce David, for leaving me, thus setting me off on this transformational journey.

Last, but certainly not least, I have used quotations from the *Tao te Ching* at the beginning of each chapter. I've done so not because it represents my own spiritual path, but because it expresses the deep universal Truths in a uniquely Chinese way. Even though there is very little spiritual practice currently in the country, it is an ancient stream underlying the culture, perhaps waiting to be awakened. The quotes have been taken, with permission, from the Stephen Mitchell translation.

About the Author

Susan Straight has been a leader in the service learning movement in the U.S. since 1994 and has promoted volunteerism internationally since 2000 in Japan, Thailand, Argentina, Australia, and then for eight years in China. Her passion is to inspire and empower young people to take an active role in solving many of the world's problems, assuming a deeper responsibility.

Susan has trained teachers, developed student projects, promoted service learning at the NM legislature and in Washington, DC, and created a structure for university volunteering in Yunnan Province, China. In addition, she has created cross-cultural programs between the United States and China, bringing university students together to assist in alleviating poverty in Yunnan Province's minority villages. The Center for Intercultural Education, which Ms. Straight leads, supports students in running their own projects, learning project management, volunteer management, financial management, marketing and promotion, and grant writing. All of the Chinese programs have been student run.

Ms. Straight has divided her time between Santa Fe, New Mexico in the United States and Kunming, Yunnan, China, but is currently residing in the U.S.

To learn more about the Center for Intercultural Education please access the website at:

www.centerinterculturaled.org

To participate in any of the Center's programs or to make a donation to the organization or any of its projects, click on the donate button found on the website or contact

centerinterculturaled@gmail.com.

All donations to the Center are tax deductible.

Book Notes

An Invitation to Serve

Many people who read a book like this and who are moved by what is presented, might find themselves wondering whether they, too, could have experiences like those presented here, or how they might create a more meaningful life. Yet, since they have no idea HOW to actually go about doing it, they might then just move on to the NEXT book.

But that could be a great loss, to both that reader, and to the world.

If you have been moved by something in this book and want to pursue a change in your own life, I am here to encourage you—to tell you that you CAN actually do it. The world is changing; and because it is, service and community have never been more important. Service and community have been threads running continuously throughout the tapestry of my life, and it was by being willing to follow those threads—wherever they led—that I discovered the work I was to do in China. Perhaps something like this is true for you, too. Or if not, you might want to add a new color to your existing tapestry. What is your contribution to this new world? If this book inspires you, consider becoming part of the dialogue.

There are three ways to do so:

- Engage in a process of visioning and self-discovery
- Seek more information
- Work with me

Self-Discovery: Is this for You?

I invite you to explore possibilities for more involvement in our changing world. You might begin by asking yourself what your own unique contribution to the world might be. Sometimes there are clues to be found in looking at what social issue you feel most passionate about: is it, for example, hunger, housing, or perhaps education?

Sometimes we are called to work in foreign lands with cultures unfamiliar to us; other times, we need look no further than our own communities. What issues or actions are right in front of you, just asking to be done?

Below are some questions to help you think about what next steps you might wish to take:

1. Do you feel you are at a crossroads in your life? We live at a time of rapid change. In order to help this movement toward a more connected and loving world, each of us must also change. In a sense, we are *all* at a crossroads. The question then becomes: which way do YOU want to go?
2. Would you say that your life is deeply meaningful?
3. What were you passionate about when you were a child? Have you pursued it or has it lain dormant? Do you want to pursue it now?
4. Are you interested in other cultures? If so, which ones?
5. What do you think your unique gifts are? Who could benefit from them?
6. If you had a magic wand and could have the world be any way you want it to be, what would that world look like?

How would people be interacting with each other?

7. What do you think the major issues in the world are? Could you do anything to help?

Seek More Information

I have created a monthly newsletter for readers so they can continue to hear about moving volunteer experiences, new programs being offered, volunteer travel programs, classes and internships in countries around the world. To register to receive this newsletter, go to the website www.centerinterculturaled.org and click on the button that says "Newsletter." We honor your privacy and will not sell our newsletter list to others.

Work with Me

- If you are interested in personal coaching to help you move toward a more involved and meaningful life, I can work with you one-on-one or in small groups to help you discover your path.

Or

- If you are part of a non-profit organization looking for new and more dynamic directions, the Center has created a new potential structure for NGOs and volunteers based on vision, empowerment and an organic rather than linear approach to growing the organization. This is available for replication.

To explore any of these possibilities, you can email me directly at centerinterculturaled@gmail.com.

Footnotes:

1. *Tao te Ching, An Illustrated Journey*, translated by Stephen Mitchell, published by HarperCollins, 1998:
Chapter 1: #12 paragraph 2 lines 1-2
Chapter 2: #74 paragraph 1 lines 1-2
Chapter 3: #10 paragraph 1, lines 4-5
Chapter 4: #27 paragraph 1 line 1, paragraph 2 lines 1-2
Chapter 5: #23 paragraph 3 lines 1-2
Chapter 6: #35 paragraph 1
Chapter 7: #45 paragraph 3 lines 1-2
Chapter 8: #51 paragraph 2 lines 1-4
Chapter 9: #52 paragraph 4 lines 1-2
Chapter 10: #81 paragraph 2 lines 1-3
Chapter 11: #65 paragraph 3 lines 4-6
Chapter 12: #64 paragraph 2 lines 3-4
Chapter 13: #13 paragraph 4 lines 3-4
Chapter 14: #50 paragraph 1 line 1, line 3
Chapter 15: #64 paragraph 4 line 6
Chapter 16: #47 paragraph 1 line 1
Chapter 17: #68 paragraph 1 line 4 lines 7-8
Chapter 18: #63 paragraph 1 last 2 lines
Chapter 19: #2 paragraph 3 lines 4-5
Chapter 20: #77 paragraph 3 line 1
Epilogue: #61 paragraph 1 lines 4-5

2. Vision, visioning: A bit like imagination, though with the quality of inner clarity or a clear view of the way things could be. In the context of the book, the three visions came to me more from a spiritual realm than from my own imagination. They

were a surprise to me at the time as they seemed to come out of nowhere, but they were also extremely clear and detailed. The use of the term "visioning" refers to a process that has been developed to assist an individual or group to "tap into" an inner vision or a very high possibility for the future. If a group, the process then helps the group to create a shared vision. The process then helps individuals and groups to identify the actions that will help to bring forth their vision in the world.

3. Explanation of the Tao: The Tao is often thought of as the all-encompassing source from which all flows into this world. In other traditions, it might be thought of as God, Allah, or the Great Mystery.

4. Many Chinese people have chosen English names to make it easier for foreigners to pronounce. All English sounding names used in the book refer to Chinese people, other than those in the acknowledgements and my partner Bruce, mentioned in the beginning of the book.

46547159R00116

Made in the USA
San Bernardino, CA
10 March 2017